# DREAM BUILDER

# DREAM
# BUILDER

For we are God's masterpiece. He has created us anew in Christ Jesus, so we can do the good things he planned for us long ago. —*Ephesians 2:10 NLT*

## ALIENE THOMPSON

info@treasuredministries.com
www.TreasuredMinistries.com

To Josh and Justin.

You are a gift in my life beyond measure.

# CONTENTS

*Corresponding Dream Builder Video Series and resources
for leaders available online.
Visit www.nourishbiblestudyseries.com*

# ACKNOWLEDGMENTS

To my family . . .

My son Justin found a piece of red sea glass on the beach last summer, three weeks after a hurricane hit the North Carolina shores. If you have read *You Belong to the Bridegroom*, you know why sea glass has a special place in my heart. In this study, a woman shares her story to show that, just as broken pieces of sea glass can be vessels of beauty, God takes the broken things of our life and makes them beautiful.

I love this imagery and have become a collector of sea glass treasures tossed on our North Carolina shores. Storms often dredge such treasures from the depths and cast them to the shore. Each piece of sea glass is a treasure, but red sea glass is the rarest treasure of all.

Not so long ago, I walked through a storm of hurricane proportions. I wanted to quit Treasured Ministries. I didn't want to write one more word. But because of my family who loved me despite my imperfections and pointed me to His perfection, I was able to get back up again and move on.

*I found my greatest treasure in my family. The unconditional love I share with my husband Jim and my two boys Josh and Justin is my rarest treasure. Three beautiful pieces of spectacular red sea glass.*

Through their compassion, I learned more about what real love is—it is giving with no motive attached. This love compels me to continue the work God has given me through Treasured Ministries. With their support, I found the courage to write again. They didn't see my past problems—they saw this potential: Jesus takes the broken things in our life and makes them beautiful.

# HOW TO USE THE
# *NOURISH BIBLE STUDY SERIES*

### 1 WATCH THE INTRODUCTION VIDEO TO BEGIN.

The introduction video is designed to give you inspiration and a foundation for your journey ahead. Video session notes pages are provided to give you a way to journal while you watch.

### 2 READ CHAPTER ONE AND THEN WATCH THE CORRESPONDING VIDEO FOR THE CHAPTER.

Following chapter one, you will watch video session one. Continue to repeat this process with the remaining chapters of the Nourish Bible Study Series and discover truth for the life you were created to live.

### 3 EXPERIENCE THE LIFE-CHANGING EFFECTS OF GOD'S WORD.

You can gain the courage, confidence, direction, and freedom to become all God created you to be. And God's words—not the words you hear from others, but God's words—are the keys to unlocking this door. Uncover your full potential to live out your purpose as you make room for the Holy Spirit to speak to your heart and discover God's timeless truth for real issues women face today.

### NOTE: An option to consider for a lighter load

Looking for a lighter load for weekly study? One solution that works well for many women is to simply divide each chapter in half and complete just three days of study each week instead of all six. This way, each chapter will take two weeks to complete. That's fine—there's no deadline. Use this method if it helps you create the margin necessary to get the most out of your study without sacrificing any content.

*Corresponding Dream Builder Video Series and resources for leaders available online.*
*Visit www.nourishbiblestudyseries.com*

# VIDEO SESSION NOTES

**Introduction Session**
DREAM BUILDER
*Acts 2:17*

Videos located online at www.nourishbiblestudyseries.com

# Chapter 1
# THE DREAM

# DAY 1

He made me into a polished arrow and concealed me in his quiver.
—*Isaiah 49:2*

My mentor's face reflected the quiet strength of Jesus. Her nurturing soul filled her living room with an atmosphere of trust, inviting me to stop pretending. I was relieved. My body relaxed. Tears began.

"What's wrong, Aliene?"

Pretending is exhausting and prevents healing. Honesty before God and healing always walk hand in hand. However, I had tried so hard to keep those painful feelings at bay by pretending everything was OK. But everything was not OK. I was not OK.

I was mourning the loss of a dream. When that dream shriveled and fell to the ground, I felt as if a part of me had died. I felt like a total failure, as if God had abandoned me. But pride wouldn't let me admit to others or myself how much this loss had impacted my identity. And so I pretended.

But not today. Today, an avalanche of emotions that I had been shoving down began to flow with such force that they pushed right through my self-protective barrier of denial. My mentor held my hands and let me cry. Her authenticity allowed me to remove my mask and open up a door to my soul. I began to answer her questions about the hurtful details of the past year, including how God had made it clear to me that I was to walk away from the large women's Bible study I led.

One of the greatest privileges in my life at that time was building, teaching, and leading this group of women. Over time, though, that dream had become larger in my life than the Dream Builder, more important to me than God, and had assumed such a large position in my life that it was robbing me of my relationship with God and creating confusion and failure.

My work for God had become greater than my worship of God.

My pot—my purpose—had become greater than the Potter.

My identity had shifted its source from Jesus to ministry success.

My ministry to my church had taken priority over my ministry to my family.

My misplaced priorities had created wrong choices.

I shared this story with my mentor that day, although my uncontrollable sobs interrupted my sentences. Was I making sense at all? But in her eyes, I could see that my mentor understood completely and that she had been there too. She understood my pain in feeling that, having given up my Bible-teaching ministry, I was now living without purpose. Her validation of my feelings gave me permission to begin processing my emotions so I could start a journey toward truth.

Where did the steady wisdom built into her instruction come from? From years of living and from love of God's Word. She always held both love and truth in her hands in such a way that you couldn't tell where one began and the other ended. Today was no exception.

After listening to my story intently, she spoke truth as one who had fought this battle before. "Giving your heart to Jesus is a costly choice, but it's one he created you for, Aliene. Jesus wants to be more than your Savior—he also wants to be Lord of your heart and of your future. He wants to build a dream through you, but when the dream becomes larger than the Dream Builder, your heart cannot be fully his, and the dream cannot be all that God has designed it to be. The Lord prunes those he loves to create a greater harvest for his glory."

The tattered pages of her well-worn Bible turned effortlessly to Isaiah 49:1–4:

> Listen to me, you islands;
>     hear this, you distant nations:
> Before I was born the LORD called me;
>     from my mother's womb he has spoken my name.
> He made my mouth like a sharpened sword,
>     in the shadow of his hand he hid me;
> he made me into a polished arrow
>     and concealed me in his quiver.
> He said to me, "You are my servant,
>     Israel, in whom I will display my splendor."
> But I said, "I have labored in vain;
>     I have spent my strength for nothing at all.
> Yet what is due me is in the LORD's hand,
>     and my reward is with my God."

"Do you know what's happening in your life now, what's causing all of this discomfort?" she asked. "He's putting you back into his quiver, close to his heart, where you can heal and your heart can become fully his. An expert archer keeps his arrows in his quiver, close to him, so that he can sharpen and polish them, releasing them again and again with power, purpose, and precision. Like the expert archer, God is calling you to retreat into his presence so he can prepare and position your heart to be released for his glory."

She reached into her drawer, pulled out a copy of *Streams in the Desert*, and gave it to me. In the days to come, as I prayerfully read through it, I would learn that the hearts of believers who had walked before me had all been broken at some time in their lives. Their stories let me know that I was not alone.

## Dreams and Joseph

In this book, we'll be looking at the story of Joseph, one of the Bible's most indelible characters. My prayer is that as we look at his story, you too will find hope. His life was full of trials, but God's dream for his life prevailed. Indeed, many of his trials became stepping stones that the Dream Builder used to accomplish his will in Joseph's life.

To every woman out there who has lost her ability to hope, to dream: I have been there. This study is just for you.

A God-ordained dream never truly dies. God's dreams were designed before we were born, to bring him glory (Ephesians 2:10). God places those desires in our hearts as seeds to stir our hearts for a harvest. Often it is the adversity in our lives that tills the soil of our hearts in such a way as to provide a greater harvest, as we are pushed to depend solely on Jesus.

However, it is this very adversity that the enemy of our souls uses to capsize the dream. The enemy's lies are not merely an attack on the dream, they are an attack on our very identity as a child of God designed for a purpose. Satan capitalizes on our catastrophe by feeding us lies about the goodness of God, about ourselves, and about the dream.

Sometimes we stop dreaming. Hope fades. God becomes smaller. The fear of stepping out again masquerades as humility.

And when this happens, we all lose out, because every woman's purpose is a part of God's plan. She was created and designed to bring value to this world and to bring glory to God as she walks in her purpose.

Like God, we too have dreams. Not all of those dreams become reality, but a dream that dies may not be lost. It can also be the birthing ground for God to build his dream through us.

The Dream Builder is a rebuilder.

Our brokenness becomes beautiful.

Our pain becomes our purpose.

Our mistake becomes our message.

Our rejection becomes God's redirection.

Our failure becomes his foundation to build.

*Sometimes our dreams have to fall to the ground to create a greater harvest.*

It can be a long time between when a seed falls and when you begin to see the harvest. For me, that time was painful. I questioned my faith. I questioned God's love for me. Life felt hopeless. That dark cloud of depression settled over my soul as the enemy whispered lies in my ear. I thought my dream was over.

But my losing became gaining. God was leading me through the painful process of purifying my heart so that the seed could yield a greater harvest—one for his glory.

My race had only just begun. It was in getting back up that my faith was strengthened and my relationship with God deepened.

Only God can orchestrate the way the brokenness of our lives allows him to build his dream through us. Step by step, God has continued to heal my own wounds so that I am free to live as God intended. And these steps, these journeys and milestones he has led me through, spill over into every word I write for Treasured Ministries—like the words on this page. These words are stones my Dream Builder uses as I write from a surrendered heart.

The Dream Builder is a rebuilder, and he builds on the foundation of a surrendered heart. Brave heart, it is time to dream again.

## The Dare

I dare you.

I dare you to move into your God-given dream. I dare you to live the adventure—the adventure you begin by listening to the Holy Spirit. I dare you to lose your life—yourself—and find what is important: loving God with your whole heart and, from that overflow, giving his love to others.

I dare you to believe in the dream again. The dream God whispered into your heart when you became his. The dreams that found their way into those places you pretended as a little girl. The desires he placed in your heart.

I dare you to step out and become the woman God created you to be.

I dare you to redefine success by measuring it in faithfulness.

I dare you to let God build that dream for you by stepping into complete surrender to his will. I dare you to pray dream-sized prayers again. And I dare you to let go of the outcome of those prayers by holding your dream loosely so that God can shape it into what it needs to be.

If you've fallen, I dare you to get back up again and finish your race, armed with a growth mindset that flows from grace and the humility to run your race in complete dependence on God's strength.

I dare you to walk in step with your God-given destiny.

What is your dream? Only when we lay our dreams at the feet of Jesus in complete surrender will we find freedom and the real joy that comes only from trusting Jesus as Lord over our lives. Your Dream Builder will meet your deepest needs at the place of greatest surrender. *Onward.* You matter. Your purpose matters. Don't give up. Instead, give in, and watch God build his dream through you.

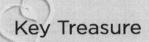

## Key Treasure

Sometimes our dreams have to fall to the ground to create a greater harvest.

# DAY 2

Whether you turn to the right or to the left, your ears will hear a voice behind you, saying, "This is the way; walk in it." —*Isaiah 30:21*

Joseph was a dreamer. He not only *had* dreams—he could interpret them too. He embraced them. By living his dreams—his God-designed dreams—he saved the lives of many.

His story is your story too. Your dream will be different, but just like Joseph, you are here for a purpose greater than yourself.

Joseph is often remembered as one who wore a rainbow. Beautiful, multicolored brilliance cascaded over his shoulders and down his sleeves. His coat of many colors was a generous gift from Jacob, his father. It was also a flagrant display of this father's favoritism toward his seventeen-year-old son. Putting on that glorious garment each morning must have reminded Joseph of his father's great love. But the richly ornamented robe was also a thorn in the side of his eleven brothers, a constant reminder that Joseph was the favorite.

One night Joseph had a dream, and then another a few nights later. The dreams showed him in a position of power and greatness. He would become so great that even his brothers and his father would bow down to him. He told his family about the dreams, and the envy brewing in his brothers' hearts finally spilled over.

They tossed Joseph into a pit.

The brothers' intent was evil, but the pit would propel Joseph into God's purpose. His brothers' betrayal activated his adventure of living the dream God had given him. That dream, after all, was not Joseph's alone—it was also God's dream. It was God who had created that dream in Joseph's mind as he slept. And when God designs a dream, he opens a door that no one can shut (Revelation 3:8; Acts 5:38–39).

Nor was this a brand-new dream. The door leading to Joseph's dream had actually opened many years before, when God gave a vision and spoke a promise to Joseph's great-grandfather, Abraham. Joseph's dream was part of the fulfillment of his great-grandfather's dream. So before we follow Joseph in this adventure, let's first trace the roots of his dream. We will meet not only Abraham but also Isaac and Jacob, Joseph's grandfather and father. These three men are considered the patriarchs of God's chosen nation.

## Tracing Joseph's Roots—and Ours

Abraham was a father to many. Read Galatians 3:6–9. According to verse 7, who are the children of Abraham?

_____

_____

_____

_____

The remarkable truth is that through faith in Christ, you can be grafted into Abraham's family (Romans 11:17). Joseph's roots are not his alone—they also belong to all who believe in Jesus. You have a stake in your family heritage of faith.

Abram (his name until God later changed it to Abraham) began his journey with the Lord in his seventies. Comfortably nested in the town of Ur, Abram had made a name for himself. He had riches and a beautiful wife named Sarai. He belonged to a prosperous family. He worshiped many gods (as was the custom) because he had never heard of the one true, living God. But all of that was about to change. On an ordinary day, God was getting ready to do the extraordinary. God, who had spoken the world into creation, would speak to Abram and make him and Sarai into a great nation—God's chosen people.

The LORD had said to Abram, "Go from your country, your people and your father's household to the land I will show you.

"I will make you into a great nation,
    and I will bless you;
I will make your name great,
    and you will be a blessing.
I will bless those who bless you,
    and whoever curses you I will curse;
and all peoples on earth
    will be blessed through you."

So Abram went, as the LORD had told him; and Lot went with him. Abram was seventy-five years old when he set out from Harren. (Genesis 12:1–4)

Abram left his family, his religion, and his country—everything familiar to him—to pursue this new voice speaking to his heart louder than any other.

What was it about the words God spoke to Abram that made such an impact in his life? Abram had plenty of gods, money, family, and fame; yet the words God spoke to him would change his life, the lives of those around him, and the lives of everyone to come. Permanently leaving home was unheard of in Abram's culture. Abram had every tangible reason to stay where he was, but God made him some big and compelling promises that were just interesting enough to propel him forward into his dream. God offered Abram a deep significance he had never imagined before, but to get it, he would have to walk away from the security and provision he had built for himself and trade them in for God's provision. Abram had no way of knowing that God would provide—he walked by faith (Genesis 15:6; Romans 4:3).

God's words were life-changing because Abram chose to listen and follow them.

Following Jesus is not a method; it is a way of life. The Dream Builder wants all his children to walk through the door of their God-given dreams, but he may give each one a different path to follow. Our breakthrough comes when we stop, listen, and follow God's leading in our lives. That's why a personal relationship with Jesus Christ is so important: God's dream is revealed through our relationship with him.

## Abram Chose to Listen to God—and to Follow Him

Abram's forefathers gave him a religion of false gods and untruths. His family probably presented convincing arguments as to why he should not leave his traditions, his false gods, his prominent position in the community, and his family to follow God's voice. Abram could have listened to them. But he didn't. He chose to listen to the one true, living God. He chose to follow the dream God had given him.

Abram listened to God's voice. Because he listened, he established a nation that would be a channel of blessing to all people. Through Abram's descendants, the Messiah would come and bring forgiveness and life to all who would join the family of faith. If Abram had listened to other voices, the outcome would have been quite different. Although he made plenty of mistakes and missteps along the way, Abram continued to listen to God, and God was faithful to build his dream through this man of faith.

Just as God knew all about Abram, he knows all about you. Just as he gave a dream to Abram, God has a dream—a calling—for your life. Are you ready to listen and live out your unique purpose?

> The Lord spoke to Abram in a vision. Jesus came to earth to dwell with humanity. How does God lead us today? Read Galatians 3:14 and John 16:13–15.

Read Jeremiah 29:11; Psalm 32:8; Acts 1:4–8; 1 Corinthians 3:9–16. Why do you think it's vital to allow the Holy Spirit to lead and guide you to your purpose?

_____

_____

_____

_____

## The Holy Spirit Will Lead You

Joseph inherited the blessing given to Abraham, and as children of Abraham, we too are blessed by the new covenant. A blessed truth of the new covenant is that the Holy Spirit can lead us.

You see, if God is the Dream Builder, then we need to seek him for the blueprints of our lives (Jeremiah 29:11). The Dream Builder is not bound by the dreams we create; he moves us according to his plan, which can sometimes lead us in new directions (Mark 7:8).

The Holy Spirit lives inside every believer and speaks to us every day, everywhere. One primary way the Spirit speaks to us is through God's written Word, which is alive and active (Hebrews 4:12). There is a relationship between God's Word and the Holy Spirit (Ephesians 6:17; John 1:1; 2 Timothy 3:16). As you keep in step with the Holy Spirit, you will find the pathway to God's destiny for your life.

Right on the heels of the Gospels, the book of Acts is filled with adventure as believers follow the leadership of the Holy Spirit. Motivated by God's love, the early church moved, keeping in step with the Spirit—and their lives impacted others. The apostles listened and followed the promptings of the Holy Spirit, and God accomplished the amazing.

God has not changed. The Holy Spirit who indwelled and empowered the early church still lives inside every believer. God is still the Dream Builder. God has a dream for *you* and a plan for that dream. Each step he gives you as your dream unfolds is like another thread in an unfolding tapestry of God's design.

## God Has a Dream for You

When Abram listened to the Lord, the experience was life-changing. When you believe God will speak to you—not just to Abram or Joseph, not just to the disciples or the apostles—it will be a turning point for you too.

Abram's obedience to God's voice allowed God's blessings to flow to him and through him to others. The nation of God's chosen people began through one man saying yes to God's voice.

Moment-by-moment choices will frame your world. Whom will you allow to write your story? Take the pen and place it in the Author's hand by surrendering to his words so he can shape your soul.

You are blessed to be a blessing. God wants to plant a dream in your heart. This is your heritage; this is your future. It was Joseph's story, and it is also your story. God is a Dream Builder, and he will lead you into your unique destiny as you listen to and follow the Holy Spirit.

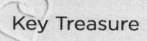

## Key Treasure

The Dream Builder wants all his children to walk through the door of their God-given dreams, but he may give each one a different path to follow. Our breakthrough comes when we stop, listen, and follow God's leading in our lives.

# DAY 3

The LORD will vindicate me; your love, LORD, endures forever.
—*Psalm 138:8*

I needed to clear the cluttered thoughts in my head, so I set my writing aside and headed outside for a walk. It was June and I was on a retreat at the coast, where I could pull away in preparation for writing this study. That particular day, careless words cast my way invited worry into my heart. I made the mistake of replaying the reckless words repeatedly in my head. Fearful thoughts began their persuasive, persistent parade in my mind. I allowed them to stay. Doubt made its debut, and I began to question God's promises to me concerning a new direction in my writing. My focus shifted off God's faithfulness and onto myself.

## God Is More than Enough

As I found my way to the seashore that night, the beauty of the beach lifted my heavy heart up to God's arms. The pounding of waves rolling to reach the shoreline soothed my soul. At each step, the sand surrounded my feet and pushed up between my toes. Like diamonds tossed on a blanket of black velvet, the stars scattered across the dark sky were breathtaking. The sound of waves, the sensation of sand, and the sight of God's shimmering, starlit sky interrupted my thoughts from their destructive cycle as I realized I was surrounded by God's faithfulness. The stars reminded me of God's promise to Abram.

> "A son who is your own flesh and blood will be your heir." He took him outside and said, "Look up at the sky and count the stars—if indeed you can count them." Then he said to him, "So shall your offspring be." (Genesis 15:4–5)

Underneath the starry sky on the beach that night, I was reminded that the One who hung the stars in the sky is also the One whose strength would supply what I needed in order to serve him. How would I be able to take this next step in the pathway of purpose? The answer came from my heart with a verse I had hidden there by memory. Just before I wrote *Brave Heart*, the very first Bible study in the Nourish Bible Study Series, the Lord gave me this promise to hold on to: "The LORD will vindicate me; your love, LORD, endures forever" (Psalm 138:8). I repeated the promise over and over—and hope and faith began to glimmer again like a new, flickering star.

## Promise Keeper

Promises are a vital part of God's provision as he builds our dreams. Our faith is like a bridge between God's promises and his provision.

God would provide everything Abram needed to follow the plan. God told Abram he would bless him, make his name great, and would be on his side when things went wrong. He added other amazing promises besides.

When the Dream Builder gives you a dream, he will also give you the means to accomplish it, whether or not you realize it at first. Sometimes the fulfillment of those promises is immediate, but other times, when God gives us a promise, we must wait for the actual provision to arrive. It's important to hold these promises in our hearts while we wait on God's perfect timing to see them fulfilled.

Dwelling on God's promises instead of your problems anchors your heart to hope to keep you steady and steadfast in your purpose as you wait for God's provision.

## From Faith to Fear and Back Again

Time passed, and Abram and Sarai weren't getting any younger. Still they saw no signs of a son from their own flesh and blood. As they waited, their faith wavered. Because beliefs determine behaviors, their doubts drove them to take matters into their own hands, deviating from God's plan. At Sarai's request, Abram, then eighty-six, slept with his servant Hagar, and she conceived a son they named Ishmael. It was not uncommon during this time in history for a man to sleep with a servant to grow his family. Hagar and Abram most likely thought they were helping achieve God's dream for him. However, this choice would reap negative consequences, causing havoc in Abram's home front and for God's chosen people for generations to come (Genesis 16:6–16; 21:8–21; Galatians 6:7–8).

Although they were still pointed in the direction of God's dream when they chose to involve Hagar, Abram and Sarai went outside God's plan. God had specifically told Abram that his family would come from his line. But I would be embarrassed to point my finger at Abram, since in my haste to make things happen, I've sometimes been guilty of trying to play Holy Spirit. Every time I do, I regret it.

When unbelief enters our thinking, it can cause our minds to swing from faith to fear. Abram still struggled with doubt. Even though God continued to speak to him through the years, confirming his promise, Abram could not grasp how Sarai could have a baby in her old age.

However, Abram's failure was not final. The Dream Builder is a rebuilder. God began to build Abram's faith by continuing to remind him of his promise to Abram through his spoken word. When Abram was ninety-nine, the Lord appeared to him again.

> Abram fell facedown, and God said to him, "As for me, this is my covenant with you: You will be the father of many nations. No longer will you be called Abram; your name will be Abraham, for I have made you a father of many nations. I will make you very fruitful; I will make nations of you, and kings will come from you." (Genesis 17:3–6)

During this same encounter, God changed Sarai's name to Sarah, declaring that she would become the mother of many nations.

Walking by faith isn't natural. In fact, Abraham first fell facedown and later laughed. "Will Sarah bear a child at the age of ninety?" (Genesis 17:17). It seemed out of the question. Sarah too laughed at the Lord. Both Sarah and Abraham had their eyes on their own ability instead of God's.

## Dwelling on God's Promises Instead of Problems

Over the years God continued to renew Abraham's mind by repeating his promises to him, like waves constantly crashing on the seashore. God was not simply building a dream—he was building Abraham's faith.

At some point in this journey, Abraham's faith strengthened beyond doubt. The laughter ceased, and he never looked back. He also stopped looking within. Abraham was looking up, and his faith was strengthened as he dwelled on God's promises instead of his own problems.

> Without weakening in his faith, he faced the fact that his body was as good as dead—since he was about a hundred years old—and that Sarah's womb was also dead. Yet he did not waver through unbelief regarding the promise of God, but was strengthened in his faith and gave glory to God, being fully persuaded that God had power to do what he had promised. (Romans 4:19–21)

One day, God's promise became a reality. Sarah gave birth to Isaac. This baby was the evidence of God's faithfulness to his promise, and a miracle so unbelievable that Sarah remarked that people would laugh when they heard the news.

The name *Isaac* means "laughter" or "he laughs." Let his life remind you that often God will give us a promise so humanly impossible that others may laugh at us if we are not already laughing ourselves. Human effort brought about Ishmael's birth; God's promise resulted in Isaac's miraculous birth. Our Dream Builder is the ultimate promise keeper (Galatians 3:3; 4:23–25).

## The Next Step in God's Plan

As Abraham grew older, his thoughts turned to the future. It was time for Isaac to marry. Fully committed to God's vision, Abraham sought his servant's help to find Isaac a wife. Finding one from his own clan of people, especially after moving far away, was a step in the plan that would bring new challenges. But this time Abraham was not laughing; he was fully persuaded that God would provide a bride for Isaac and continue to build his dream.

After hearing God's promises spoken to him repeatedly, Abraham had the words hidden in his heart. This time the Lord did not have to speak to him to remind him of his promises—Abraham declared the words himself: "The LORD, the God of heaven, who brought me out of my father's household and my native land and who spoke to me and *promised* me on oath, saying, 'To your offspring I will give this land'—he will send his angel before you so that you can get a wife for my son from there" (Genesis 24:7, *emphasis mine*).

## God Provided—Again

God was faithful again. The story of Isaac and Rebekah is simply a sweet one to savor. Read Genesis 24:34–67 and answer the questions below.

What evidence can you find that Abraham's faith was contagious with his servant and his son Isaac?

_____

_____

_____

Note the characteristics of the servant's prayer—are there some characteristics that you would like to bring into your own prayer lives? What role do God's promises and provision and our faith play in our prayer lives?

_____

_____

_____

Verse 63 tells us that Isaac meditated. When and where did Isaac meditate? What do you think he was meditating on?

_____

_____

_____

Abraham's servant walked with faith like Abraham's as he went out to find a bride for Isaac. The servant prayed specifically, simply, and with absolute assurance. Let the servant's prayer inspire you to pray bold, simple, but specific prayers filled with faith in God's promises to accomplish the "how" in your dream. In response to the servant's faith-filled prayer, God led him directly to Isaac's new bride, Rebekah.

Abraham's faith was also found in the surrendered heart of his son Isaac. While he was waiting for the servant to return with his new bride, Isaac, instead of doubting and worrying, "went out to the field one evening to meditate" (Genesis 24:63). I believe he sat and gazed at the stars, prompting his thoughts to rest on God's faithfulness as he meditated on the promise given to Abraham.

After meditating, he looked up and saw camels approaching. On one camel was a woman named Rebekah, who would carry on the important lineage of Abraham's blessing. The Bible says Isaac loved Rebekah. They quickly married. Before Abraham died, he saw his son of promise marry. He died in peace, knowing that his dream—God's dream—would continue.

God is ever faithful to his word—always.

What promises has God given you? Are you in a season of waiting to see those promises come to pass? While we patiently wait and believe, we would be wise to pray persistently for the fulfillment of those promises. Prayer is the key to keeping our hope alive and our steps aligned with his Word. Meditating on those promises will help you to walk by faith and not by sight and to remain steadfast on your journey to becoming the woman God created you to be.

# DAY 4

Show me your ways, LORD, teach me your paths. Guide me in your truth and teach me, for you are God my Savior, and my hope is in you all day long. —*Psalm 25:4–5*

As our story continues, Rebekah and Isaac are going to have a baby ... or two (Genesis 25:19–28).

I imagine a smile blazed across Isaac's face when his beautiful wife told him she was pregnant. She had been barren, but the Dream Builder answered their prayers. Rebekah not only carried twins, but she also carried the future of God's chosen people. She was essentially pregnant with God's dream.

When the twins jostled inside Rebekah, the storm she experienced within concerned her. The Bible says Rebekah went to inquire of the Lord: "Why is this happening to me?" God spoke to Rebekah and gave her a blueprint—or prophecy—for the future.

> The LORD said to her, "Two nations are in your womb, and two peoples from within you will be separated; one people will be stronger than the other, and the older will serve the younger." (Genesis 25:23)

Rebekah gave birth to fraternal twins, Jacob and Esau. Esau was born first, with Jacob literally grasping the heel of his brother as he arrived seconds later. Although Esau was technically born first and therefore, by tradition, would be the recipient of the blessing, God revealed to Rebekah that the younger son, Jacob, would actually inherit the blessing.

> Although God foreknew that this would happen, the Bible points out clearly that Esau willingly traded his birthright. Read Genesis 25:29–34; 27:27–34 and Hebrews 12:14–17. For what did Esau trade his birthright?

Before you look down on Esau, remember that *you've got a "stew" too*. Like Esau's hunger for stew, healthy desires can quickly turn into unhealthy demands that destroy our ability to make wise decisions. All of us have desires that can overtake our thoughts and actions. The enemy uses these desires like buttons to push us in a direction we don't want to travel. Beware: If Satan used Jesus' hunger to try to tempt him in the wilderness, he will use our appetites to tempt us as well. (Matthew 4:1–4)

What is your appetite—your "stew"? What do you think you need in order to feel secure, happy, significant, and accepted? What are you hungry for?

_____

_____

_____

_____

_____

Appetites that dominate our thoughts can drown out God's Word in our lives. Focusing on our desires, even healthy ones, with such intensity will anchor our thoughts in a destructive way and can suffocate our harvest. When we give in to those kinds of thoughts, they have power over our lives.

Wise women find freedom to build God's purpose with bold faith by letting go of worldly goals and seeking only heaven's reward. Courageous faith comes from looking up—from a gaze fixed on God's vision for your life.

## Vision

When Jacob and Esau grew to be men, the time came for Isaac to bestow his official blessing. Isaac called for his son Esau to prepare a meal so he could bless him.

Isaac favored Esau, but Rebekah favored Jacob. When she overheard Isaac's plan to bless Esau, she took matters into her own hands. Rebekah dressed Jacob in Esau's clothes and covered his hands with goatskins to make them hairy like Esau's. Isaac's weak, old eyes prevented him from seeing the truth. Jacob consented to his mother's plot, Isaac was deceived, and Jacob received the blessing instead of Esau (Genesis 27).

Naturally, when Esau discovered he had been cheated out of the blessing he thought was rightfully his, he was angry. I guess he forgot about the stew? Steaming with envy, he vowed to kill his brother for stealing his blessing and birthright. Rebekah told Jacob to run away to escape Esau's wrath until it subsided.

Jacob fled to preserve his life. He was away from his mother, who loved and protected him, and his father, who provided for him. He was haunted by thoughts of his brother, who hated him and was hunting him down to kill him. He had left all that was familiar. Along the journey, homesickness must have settled deep within him. Shame and remorse for stealing his brother's blessing probably played across his thoughts. Alone, afraid, ashamed, Jacob found his way to Luz. Worn out emotionally and physically from his travels, as the sun began to set, Jacob decided to rest for the night. Choosing a rugged, cold stone for his pillow—and perhaps to serve as a weapon of protection if angry Esau should appear[1]— Jacob drifted off into a restless sleep.

But Jacob was not alone. The Dream Builder had the right words at the right time for Jacob. God reached out to him through a dream and through his spoken word. With a visual and verbal reminder, Jacob was assured that God would not abandon him and would accomplish his purpose through him.

Read Genesis 28:10–22. Describe Jacob's dream. What do you think this vision meant?

_____

_____

_____

_____

Consider the words God spoke to Jacob, and put yourself in his place. Why were those the right words at the right time?

_____

_____

_____

_____

Can you remember a time when God reassured you with a verse from the Bible—the right words at the right time? Describe that time here.

_____

_____

_____

_____

From verses 18 and 19, how did Jacob mark this spot where God spoke?

_____

_____

_____

Jacob didn't simply acknowledge the dream in his mind. He marked the spot and moved with confidence instead of giving in to fear. Vision helped him put that revelation into action. Read Genesis 28:20–22. How did Jacob move immediately to put God's word into action?

_____

_____

_____

How might his actions have been different if he had been driven by fear instead of directed by God's word?

_____

_____

_____

A rush of reassuring love must have washed over weary Jacob. God knew him—all about him—and still spoke to his heart. God spoke not just any words but the exact ones Jacob needed to hear: "I am with you and will watch over you wherever you go, and I will bring you back to this land. I will not leave you until I have done what I have promised you" (Genesis 28:15). The stairway to heaven was a visual reminder that Jacob—not just Abraham or Isaac—had access to the Almighty!

Amazed, Jacob did not want to forget this moment. Knowing now that God would protect him, Jacob made his stone pillow into a pillar to mark the spot where God had spoken. He also marked this occasion by giving this place called Luz a new name: _Bethel_, which means "house of God." God had spoken to him personally—not just to his grandfather Abraham or to his father, Isaac, but to Jacob! This was worth documenting.

Centuries later, another biblical figure named Habakkuk heard a word from God uniquely tailored to his own discouraging circumstances. Read Habakkuk 2:2. What did the Lord tell the prophet to do?

_____

_____

_____

Why is it important for *you* to write down the vision God gives you and make it plain? How does doing so help you say no to satisfying an appetite and yes to answering God's call on your life? How does it affect your actions and, ultimately, activate God's purpose for your life?

_____

_____

_____

_____

Writing down God's plan, provision, and purpose for your life creates focus and reduces the intensity of any doubts we might have. Getting busy or caught up in "good things" can distract you from God's dream and dilute your energy. Writing the dream on paper helps you communicate your message to others, like the herald in the Bible verse. Keeping a list of the steps God has asked you to take, if you have a sense of what they might be, shows you a clear path and builds your faith and strength for future steps, as does recalling God's provision through thanksgiving. Reminding yourself of the "why" will keep you going forward for your purpose when the enemy whispers in your ear, "Just quit!"

List any ideas you have on how to create visual reminders of God's purpose for your life.

_____

_____

_____

_____

Journaling, writing goals, and creating vision boards are all practical ways to keep the focus on vision. Vision boards are collages of pictures that depict your dream. Journaling identifies the "footprints" of God that he has left for you in Scripture. You will begin to see a trail God is cutting just for you through untraveled territory. Writing down your goals, not just thinking about them, will give you a visual aim to live with clear direction.

At Bethel, God gave Jacob a vision to lift his eyes upward so he could move onward past his feelings of fear. Jacob put his faith into action by making a vow to establish Bethel as God's house and giving God a tenth of all he would receive. Then he continued on his journey. This action set his adventure in motion.

God has a vision for you. As you sit at the feet of Jesus, expect Bethel moments as you travel through the Scriptures. Keep them before you in a tangible way that strengthens your focus. Find freedom to build God's purpose with bold faith by letting go of worldly goals and seeking only heaven's reward. *Onward!*

# DAY 5

For you know that God paid a ransom to save you from the empty life you inherited from your ancestors. —*1 Peter 1:18 NLT*

You are doing amazingly well! We have covered so much ground. I applaud you for hanging in there with me.

In an effort to quickly capture Joseph's history through Abraham, Isaac, and today Jacob, you and I are blazing through the beginning of Israel's history at warp speed. It would be nice to stop awhile and ponder the patriarchs more deeply; however, today we are pressing on to learn about Joseph's mother, Rachel. Today you'll dive into the Scriptures and look at what life was like when Jacob was born and learn more about the woman who nurtured him in those early years.

After Jacob had his first encounter with the Lord at Bethel, he continued on his journey eastward to meet his uncle Laban and the future wife he believed he would find. Laban was Jacob's uncle on his mother's side, and he had two daughters: Rachel and Leah. "Leah had weak eyes, but Rachel had a lovely figure and was beautiful" (Genesis 29:17). Jacob was moved to tears when he met beautiful Rachel, the shepherdess. Jacob loved Rachel and quickly pledged seven years of work as a dowry to Laban in exchange for the hand of his beloved (Genesis 29:1–18).

However, Laban had another daughter and another plan. It was customary for the older daughter to marry first. Laban most likely didn't want his older daughter, Leah, to be unmarried all her life, so he deceived his nephew. After Jacob worked for seven years to marry his beloved Rachel and the wedding feast had been celebrated, Laban sent Leah in to consummate the marriage (vv. 21–22). It was simply too late when Jacob discovered the truth. His fate was sealed.

When he confronted Laban, his uncle agreed to give him Rachel's hand in marriage as well, as long as he would agree to another seven years of labor to earn her. So in the space of just over a week, Jacob found himself with two wives. Rachel he loved, but Leah did not have her husband's devotion (vv. 25–30).

I simply cannot wrap my head around these living conditions. Leah was second choice to her sister. Rachel was forced to share the man she loved. All the ingredients were there to cook up a terrible concoction of competition that would spill over into the lives of their children.

## All in the Family

"If you really want to know more about a man, take a look at his family." I heard this wise piece of advice as a young woman. And it is so true. No one would question that our background shapes our character. The people in our lives influence the way we are.

It is part of human nature to mimic the behavior we see in our parents. From learning to brush our teeth to learning how to act when we're married, we use the template for life that our parents provide. As we create our own households, it is natural to recreate the environment we were raised in. We may intentionally choose to recreate some aspects, but the majority of this mimicking is unintentional. When we practice what has been modeled for us, generational patterns are produced. Some cycles are healthy and others are unhealthy.

The patriarchs were not immune to negative family patterns. For example, Abraham and Sarah favored Isaac over Ishmael. Isaac and Rebekah each favored one child over the other. Jacob would in turn favor his wife Rachel and son Joseph over the rest of the family. This destructive pattern continued for at least two generations, resulting in family strife. While these patterns never prevented God's dream from coming to pass, they did create unnecessary discord and destruction.

## Longing Leads to Jealousy and Competition

Read Genesis 29:31–30:24. Do you identify more with Leah or Rachel? Why? How did fear play a role in their actions? How did this create fractures in the family?

_____

_____

_____

Leah longed for her husband's love, and Rachel longed to have a child. Their desperation to have what they did not have sparked a competition that motivated them to use drastic measures: As Sarah had done two generations before, they "gave" their maidservants to their husband to bear more children. While this practice was common at that time, I can't imagine how it affected their hearts or the hearts of their maidservants. One thing we will see in future chapters is that their behavior created a cycle: their children would give in to jealousy and hate.

I hear Leah's heartache, her need to be loved, and her reasoning that bearing another child could solve her problems: "Surely my husband will love me now" (Genesis 29:32). Fear of rejection drove her decisions. Leah turned her hopes and happiness over to a man and sought through her children to get the attention her heart craved.

I can identify with Rachel's jealousy—she had Jacob's love but was desperate for a child. Jealousy often develops from the fear of losing something or someone. I believe Rachel was afraid of losing her husband's love. She had always been the beauty; no one had known she was barren. Would she lose her standing as first place in her husband's heart? Did she feel threatened by her sister's fertility? Did she fear that she was viewed as the weaker sister because she couldn't have a child?

Rachel didn't have a child; Leah didn't have her husband's love. Driven by fear of rejection, their actions had a tremendous impact on everyone around them. Ironically, neither woman was ever satisfied. This is the lie that Satan feeds us: *God won't take care of you. You'll be happy when your husband is perfect. You'll finally have peace when your mother apologizes and makes up for the ways she didn't nurture you. When you get that promotion, your father will be proud and you can finally feel good about yourself.* If we give in to those fears, we will soon find that we have surrendered control by reaching out in our fear to the wrong person for the wrong rescue.

When Leah's and Rachel's need to be loved and valued was threatened, instead of turning to God for the kind of unwavering love, validation, and belonging that comes from being a daughter of the King, each woman reached for and grasped at the limited love of Jacob. This produced a wake of damage in their children's lives. Those twelve children, including Joseph, were born into a cycle of rivalry, jealousy, and insecurity.

## A New Bloodline

Today, we are going to discuss how we create new cycles by turning to God, living in the Spirit, and allowing Jesus to have the greatest impact in our lives. Researching and analyzing our families can help us understand why we are the way we are, but only the Holy Spirit can change us from the inside out. God is not merely a rule maker—he is a heart changer. Place under his care those things in your life you want to change and surrender to him, and you will find freedom. Experiencing God's love is always the pathway to surrender. As you focus on your relationship with him instead of trying to control people around you, you will find freedom to live as God intended.

While my background may influence my character, Joseph's story reminds me that it doesn't define my God-given destiny. God is the Dream Builder and the Promise Keeper.

Do these words ever go through your mind?

- This is the way it will always be.
- God could never build a dream through me.
- I am powerless over the negative cycles that keep happening in my life.

All of us have negative cycles that may feel like inescapable realities. But the reality is that we *can* break those cycles by making new choices. We *can* choose new life and new legacies for our children. God brings a solution that surpasses self-help, self-determination, and self-effort. God's solution is found in sonship. The Dream Builder not only adopts us but longs for us to live "led" as his daughters.

## Slave or Son? Fear or Faith?

Meditate on Romans 8:15–17 and answer the following questions. If possible, go to Bible-Gateway (http://biblegateway.com) and look up several translations.

What differences do you see in being led by God's Spirit versus being led by fear?

_____

_____

_____

_____

What is the connection between fear and slavery?

_____

_____

_____

_____

How do unhealthy family patterns feel like bondage?

_____

_____

_____

_____

How is being under the control of something or someone else slavery?

_____

_____

_____

_____

Remember the fear that created the negative cycles in Leah's and Rachel's lives? Destructive cycles are created by fear, but God invites you to break those cycles by living led by his Spirit, living loved as his daughter, and living free as one who is not bound by any cycle.

Negative family patterns can feel like bondage. When you say, "This is one thing about me I can never change," you are reflecting a slave mentality. We must think like a daughter of the Dream Builder by believing in his love for us and learning to trust and listen to the Holy

Spirit. Be mindful of what is influencing you. Trust your Abba Father and his great love for you. When praying, Jesus called God *Abba*, the Hebrew word for "Daddy." As God's adopted children, we have the same great privilege of calling the Creator of the universe our daddy.

God will lead you on a slow and deep journey of beautiful, internal transformation. This journey is called discipleship. It's a lifelong process directed by the Holy Spirit. Listen, follow, and watch God unravel cycle after cycle as you surrender to him. You may find it helpful to consult a Christian counselor. Cutting new paths is not easy and takes time. Cycles, even if they are destructive, feel comfortable, so moving beyond them is a process.

When we follow the promptings of the Holy Spirit through our relationship with our Dream Builder, he will give us new directions that will lead us out of our cycles to live as his child (1 Peter 1:17–19; Galatians 4:6–9; 5:1, 16–18). Our own efforts to fix our lives are often misguided, short-lived, and weak in comparison to the problems we face. But the Lord can do anything (Luke 18:27)! It's all about abiding in Christ, listening to the promptings of the Holy Spirit, following them, trusting in his strength, and receiving joy (Galatians 3:2–5; John 15:1–11). As a daughter of the Dream Builder, you have been adopted into a new family: God's family (John 1:12–16). His wisdom and love for you are completely pure, so you can trust the leading of the Holy Spirit (James 3:17; John 10:10–12, 27).

## New Beginnings

God gave Abraham a dream: that he should follow God's direction to a far-off land. Little did Abraham know that his so-far childless marriage would be the beginning of a nation of God's chosen people and that through his lineage a Messiah, a Redeemer, would be born to save the lives of many. "For God so loved the world that he gave his one and only Son, that whoever believes in him shall not perish but have eternal life" (John 3:16).

All of this happened in Abraham's life *after* he left his father's house. Your earthly father does not determine your destiny. Your heavenly Father is your Maker. Only he can determine who you are and the purpose for which you were created.

Whatever your family cycle is, know that your past does not define your future. There is hope! What you focus on will have the greatest impact on your life! Will you choose fear? Or will you choose faith in an amazing God who loves you beyond measure? If you focus on your Dream Builder and live by the Spirit, great good will come of it. Not just good for yourself, but good for touching the lives of many. Start new, healthy cycles for future generations!

# DAY 6

"People do not live by bread alone, but by every word that comes from the mouth of God." —*Matthew 4:4 NLT*

Jesus taught us in Matthew 4:4 that his revealed words are daily food, essential for nourishing our souls. Spending personal time with God to hear his word for you is not merely a goal to aspire to but also a necessary element for the health of your soul.

Ready to nourish your soul?

The Nourish Bible Study Method is a key that helps unlock truth for the life you were created to live by giving you a proven, effective, three-step approach to Bible study that connects you with Jesus. When I developed this method, I had this goal in mind:

> for every woman to be able to look at every God-inspired word in the Bible and see his truth shine through to light her path—a path that always starts with Jesus.

**Starting in chapter two,** you will begin to use the Nourish Method for the first three days of each chapter by applying one step of the Nourish Method each day to a weekly Nourish Scripture.

So, for today, I'd like to equip you for your journey by teaching you the Nourish Bible Study Method step by step.

What should you do if you are already familiar with the Nourish Bible Study Method? Simply skip this day of study, or continue reading to review and discover how the method is incorporated into each chapter of the Nourish Bible Study Series.

## *Nourish*—A Three-Step Bible Study Method to Connect with Jesus

So, let's get started!

Jesus carved out time in his day to break bread with others. Whether in an intimate setting with his disciples, a wedding celebration at Cana, a seaside fish dinner cooked over a fire with friends, or miraculously feeding thousands with five loaves and two fishes, Jesus paused to eat food with those he loved.

Think of your time with Jesus as gathering around a family dinner table he has prepared for you with much love and care.

*Reveal*, *Respond*, and *Renew* are the three steps of the Nourish Bible Study Method. Think of each step in the Nourish Bible Study Method as an ingredient in a recipe for a nourishing meal. Each ingredient is important and plays a role. Each ingredient interacts with the others. Combined, they enable you to find and understand life-giving truths in the Word that you had never seen before and nourish your soul for your journey in life.

**Here are the three steps that Nourish will lead you through:**

- **DAY 1: *Reveal.*** Connect with Jesus by studying the Scriptures and allowing the Holy Spirit to reveal truth in the Scriptures.
- **DAY 2: *Respond.*** Apply the truth using our IMPACT questions so that your life can impact the lives of those around you.
- **DAY 3: *Renew.*** Let the truth you've just learned from God's word renew your mind. Allow God to anchor his Word in your heart. Putting this life-changing discipline into your daily routine, using our practical method, will change the way you think and live.

*Reveal. Respond. Renew.* Starting next week, for the first three days of each chapter, you will take one Nourish step each day to help you take a break from the hustle and gather around the table with Jesus through the study of his Word.

Let's take a closer look at each of those three steps.

## The *Reveal* Step

### Connect with Jesus and Allow Him to Reveal Truth

There is something special about sharing a meal with others—it is more than just eating food. It is about coming together to be with one another. Gathering at the table to break bread brings pause and a place to connect.

As you carve out time to dive into Bible study and pull your chair up to the table, don't come just to read. Come to connect with Jesus by relying on the Holy Spirit to reveal his word to you.

## Switching Up Your Goal: Why Are You Studying the Bible?

What if you switched your goal from completing your study to connecting with Jesus? What if you let go of the aspiration to understand it all or do it all? What if you saw the Bible as a way to connect with your Creator instead of a way to learn a list of rules to follow? This is what the *Reveal* Step is all about.

So often, we make the mistake of coming to our table with Jesus to cross it off our to-do list rather than just to listen and let him lead and teach us. You see, God knows the nourishment need and when we need it.

Discovering the difference between diligently studying the Scriptures for information and allowing the Holy Spirit to reveal truth through those Scriptures is life-changing—because Jesus is life-changing.

**The goal of the *Reveal* Step is not to study the Scriptures solely to gain information. It is to connect with Jesus through the Bible and allow the Holy Spirit to nourish us with life-giving truth.**

### How to put the *Reveal* Step into practice during DAY 1.

**1** **PRAY.** As you begin your time in God's Word listening to Jesus, you will gain direction on becoming the woman God created you to be. Open your Bible to the weekly Nourish Scripture located at the top of the page in each chapter. Begin with prayer, asking God to speak to your heart.

**2** **JOURNAL.** Prayerfully read and reflect on the weekly Nourish Scripture. Phrases, verses, or words will catch your attention because the Holy Spirit is highlighting truth for you—mark them. Journal any thoughts you may have in the space provided for you on Day 1. Taking pen to paper will help you to process the truth God is revealing just for you.

**3** **DISCOVER.** Some days, you will simply mark up the day's passage in your Bible and journal. Other days, the Lord will prompt you to learn more about a certain word or verse or to investigate background information on the Nourish Scripture by using outside resources. Let him be your guide. For a list of some of my favorite outside resources and ways I use them as I study the Bible, download our FREE e-book, Nourishing Your Heart, at www.nourishbiblestudymethod.com.

## The *Respond* Step

### Respond to Jesus by Applying the Truth to Your Life

When God initiates the process by revealing truth and we respond to that truth, it impacts our lives and the lives around us. Holy Spirit revelation requires application for activation.

How do you study the Word in a way that *activates* the greatest *impact* in your life? You do this by *asking the right questions*.

This approach provides the focus that will help you refine the truth further and apply it more directly and profoundly to your life. That was the purpose we had in mind when we created our six IMPACT questions for this step.

### How to put the *Respond* Step into practice during DAY 2.

Return to the weekly Nourish Scripture and ask yourself the six IMPACT questions found below. What happens if some days, you can't seem to come up with an answer to all six questions? Simple—don't worry about it. If after thinking about it for a few moments, no answer to a question occurs to you, then move on to the next one.

#### IMPACT

**I**MAGE OF GOD TO TRUST? An attribute of God, Jesus, or the Holy Spirit to trust.

**M**ESSAGE TO SHARE? A word of encouragement, truth, or prayer to share.

**P**ROMISE TO TREASURE? A promise in the Bible to believe.

**A**CTION TO TAKE? A specific step God is calling you to take.

**C**ORE IDENTITY IN CHRIST TO AFFIRM? A truth about how God sees you to affirm.

**T**RANSGRESSION TO CONFESS? A sin to acknowledge for help, healing, and restoration through Christ.

Now that you know the IMPACT acronym, you know what to look for when you are studying a passage. Review the table on the next page to dive more deeply into each question so you can see why each one is important in your journey to apply the truth to your life.

## IMPACT

| | |
|---|---|
| **I**MAGE OF GOD TO TRUST? | It is important that we begin here, since what we believe about God directly affects our thoughts and actions. Attributes of God, Jesus, or the Holy Spirit can be stated directly or implied by actions in the Bible. It is eye-opening when we allow the Bible to define God's image instead of allowing our circumstances to shape how we perceive God. |
| **M**ESSAGE TO SHARE? | A message to share is a word of encouragement, truth, wisdom, or prayer from the Nourish Scripture that you feel led to give to another. It is also perhaps a message God simply wants to share with you. God's truth refreshes your soul, and when you share this with others, you will find yourself refreshed also. |
| **P**ROMISE TO TREASURE? | A promise to believe is a promise in the Bible to stand on by faith. Imagine the difference it would make in your life and the lives around you if you moved from knowing God's promises to believing them. God is ever faithful to his Word—always. |
| **A**CTION TO TAKE? | During your time in God's Word, if he prompted you to take an action step, follow through and take that step as soon as you can. Faith and action walk hand in hand. This step is all about abiding in Christ, listening to the promptings of the Holy Spirit, following them, trusting in his strength, and receiving joy (Galatians 3:2–5; John 15:1–11). Each step, small or large, creates impact. |
| **C**ORE IDENTITY IN CHRIST TO AFFIRM? | For this step, write "In Christ I am" statements that line up with the truth in God's Word. Finding your core identity in Christ is not about frantically striving to be someone, but about surrendering to God by allowing his Word to define who you are and the purpose for which you were created. This is a precious treasure to guard by faith against outside influences (what others say, our circumstances, our actions, our past, our feelings, how others treat us, worldly standards) so that you can truly give to others by embracing all God has created you to be.<br><br>Below are some examples.<br>I am God's child (John 1:12).<br>I am completely forgiven (Romans 3:21–22).<br>I am very valuable to God (Matthew 10:31).<br>I am confident in asking God for wisdom (Jeremiah 33:2–3).<br>I belong to the body of Christ (Mark 3:33–35). |
| **T**RANSGRESSION TO CONFESS? | The Holy Spirit highlights transgressions—not to condemn you, but to free you to become all God created you to be. Instead of bringing God your good behaviors (self-righteousness) or justifying, hiding, or trying to change on your own, bring your sin to God through confession. Here you will find the grace, healing, and transformation that only Christ can bring. |

## The *Renew* Step

### Renew Your Mind to Anchor the Truth in Your Heart

Have you ever left out a vital ingredient by mistake because that particular ingredient was just a small amount, but its omission had adverse effects? I think we've all been there.

Just like a dismayed contestant on the Food Network show *Chopped* who forgets a small basket ingredient because it was hiding under a dish towel, we can be disappointed with the results of our time in God's Word because we have missed a vital ingredient to weave into the fabric of our lives: *biblical meditation.*

For years, although I was deep in Bible study, I shied away from biblical meditation and missed out on a vital ingredient for soul nourishment.

> *How could just five minutes a day focusing on one verse heal me?*
> *Isn't that a New Age thing?*

I heard a lot about the importance of Bible study but nothing about biblical mediation.

### *Here's What Happened When I Added the Five-Minute Ingredient*

When I began to put God's prescription of renewing my mind into practice by starting my quiet time meditating on God's Word for just five minutes, the results were incredible.

The shift in my life personally was so profound that I decided to renovate the Nourish Method to devote one entire step to this spiritual discipline.

God does not neglect to tell us about this vital ingredient. Over and over again in the Bible, God tells his people to remember, reflect on, and renew their minds with his Word, his promises, his goodness. In fact, *meditate* is mentioned over 20 times in the Bible. This is for a good reason.

*What you think determines how you live. What you practice in your thinking determines what grows in your life.*

Just like a boat tied to its anchor, God wants our thoughts to remain steady on his truths for our lives. God alone is our anchor of truth. As an anchor exists to secure a vessel so it ceases to wander, God's Word secures our minds and hearts to him no matter what currents or waves we may face during the day.

How to put the *Renew* Step into practice during DAY 3.

**An Anchor of Truth can be one word, truth, or verse that the Holy Spirit emphasizes to you during your time in God's Word—from your Nourish Scripture or any passage in the Bible.**

**1** **SEEK GOD TO FIND YOUR ANCHOR.** Prayerfully review the weekly Nourish Scripture and the journal entries you made during the first two days. Ask God to identify for you the one anchor of truth he wants you to take away from the weekly Nourish Scripture.

**2** **RECORD YOUR ANCHOR.** Write your Anchor of Truth in the space provided on your Nourish Notes on Day 3 and on your Anchor of Truth Card. Tuck this card into your Bible or workbook just like a bookmark, so that you can be grounded in your truth daily. (Anchor of Truth cards available at www.TreasuredMinistries.com/shop.)

**3** **RENEW YOUR MIND WITH YOUR ANCHOR.** Start your daily quiet time by meditating on your Anchor of Truth. Utilizing your Anchor of Truth Card as a bookmark makes this daily habit easy! Quiet your thoughts. Focus on the truth. Read the truth. Pray the truth. Continue to reflect on your Anchor of Truth daily until the next week, when God reveals another truth to you in the course of your study.

## You're invited

The table is set, and Jesus is ready to dine with you! He has truth to nourish your soul. Carve out time to open his Word and feed your soul with the Bread of Life.

Nourish. A Bible Study Method for Life. *Reveal* > *Respond* > *Renew*.

You matter.

You're invited.

Come gather at his table!

*Learn more and use the Nourish Bible Study Method
with any of our resources, including Nourishing Your Heart,
the Nourish Notebook and 21-Day Challenge,
Nourish Bible Study Series, and Treasured Devotions.
A full list of resources can be found at
www.TreasuredMinistries.com/nourishstudies.*

# VIDEO SESSION NOTES

**Session 1**

**THE DREAM**

*Genesis 22:1-19*

Videos located online at www.nourishbiblestudyseries.com

# Chapter 2
# CALL ON HIS NAME

# DAY 1

Nourish Scripture: Genesis 32:22–32

### PRAY.
Begin your time with God in prayer.

### TAKE THE *REVEAL* STEP OF THE NOURISH BIBLE STUDY METHOD.
Connect with Jesus by studying the Weekly Nourish Scripture and allowing the Holy Spirit to reveal truth in those verses. Prayerfully read over and reflect on the passage. Mark any phrases, verses, or words that catch your attention. Journal and learn as the Lord leads you.

# DAY 2

Nourish Scripture: Genesis 32:22–32

 **PRAY.**

Begin your time with God in prayer.

## 2 TAKE THE *RESPOND* STEP OF THE NOURISH BIBLE STUDY METHOD.

Respond to activate truth in your life. The acronym **IMPACT** provides questions to help you apply the truth from your weekly Nourish Scripture.**Sometimes you may not have answers for all six questions.**

**I**MAGE OF GOD TO TRUST? An attribute of God, Jesus, or the Holy Spirit to trust.

**M**ESSAGE TO SHARE? A word of encouragement, truth, or prayer to share.

**P**ROMISE TO TREASURE? A promise in the Bible to believe.

**A**CTION TO TAKE? A specific step God is calling you to take.

**C**ORE IDENTITY IN CHRIST TO AFFIRM? A truth about how God sees you to affirm.

**T**RANSGRESSION TO CONFESS? A sin to acknowledge for help, healing, and restoration through Christ.

# DAY 3
Nourish Scripture: Genesis 32:22–32

**1 PRAY.**
Begin your time with God in prayer.

**2 TAKE THE *RENEW* STEP OF THE NOURISH BIBLE STUDY METHOD.**
Like an anchor that secures its vessel, biblical meditation secures truth to transform your life. Take five minutes to *renew* your mind by focusing on one word, verse, or truth that the Holy Spirit revealed through the Bible during your week of study. Record your truth below and on your Anchor of Truth card.* Quiet your thoughts. Focus on the truth. Read the truth. Pray the truth.

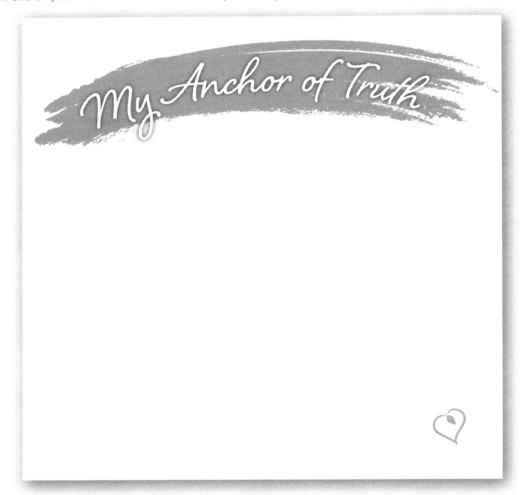

**3 UTILIZE YOUR *ANCHOR OF TRUTH* CARD AS A BOOKMARK TO CULTIVATE A DAILY PRACTICE OF BIBLICAL MEDITATION.**
Place your Anchor of Truth Card* in your Bible study workbook to bookmark tomorrow's day of study. Let your Anchor of Truth bookmark remind you to pause and renew your mind on God's Word. Repeat this process daily, continuing to reflect on your Anchor of Truth to start your quiet time until the next week, when God reveals another truth to you.

*Anchor of Truth Cards are available at www.TreasuredMinistries.com/shop

# DAY 4

Listen carefully: Unless a grain of wheat is buried in the ground, dead to the world, it is never any more than a grain of wheat. But if it is buried, it sprouts and reproduces itself many times over. In the same way, anyone who holds on to life just as it is destroys that life. But if you let it go, reckless in your love, you'll have it forever, real and eternal. —*John 12:24–25 MSG*

Sometimes our self-confidence, self-reliance, and self-dependence can be the greatest hindrance to God's plan (Romans 7:18–25). The foundation for the Dream Builder's dreams must be Jesus, because when it's anything or anyone else, even yourself, it's on shaky ground. Even our own dreams and desires can be like grains of wheat that may need to fall to the ground so new life can emerge. The Dream Builder knows you are designed for more. God wants to help you surpass your dreams to build something greater.

What do John 12:24 and John 15:2 teach us about new life?

---

---

---

---

In his great love for us, the Dream Builder pursues us and prunes us to prepare us for a new work he wants to do through us. The Dream Builder is a rebuilder. Sometimes the old has to fall away before the new can come. The Bible points to some strange truths in our created world: new comes from old, cutting back creates more, and life emerges out of death.

Certain moments of crisis or times of challenge may usher you into a new season of life, creating new energy from something that passes away. You may have a moment like this in your past, it might be happening right now, or maybe you'll have one in your future. For our study, we're calling these *rites of passage*. Contrary to the negative way we may view these difficult times, God can turn these hardships into his provision. You need never be afraid during difficulties, great though they may be; they are the labor pains for the amazing dream God is birthing through you.

## Wrestling with God

Jacob experienced an unusual rite of passage that would bring new life. Let's examine his experience to learn truths we can apply as we walk through our own rites of passage. Whether it's pruning, wrestling, or dying, know this: God is a rebuilder! His heart is to restore your life, not to destroy it. Sometimes when we feel as if we are "dying"

or "losing" or "falling," the Dream Builder is actually tearing down the old and creating something new—rebuilding something beautiful.

After twenty years in exile, it was time for Jacob to return home. During those twenty years, Jacob built a large family and prospered. Returning home meant Jacob would have to face Esau and possibly Esau's wrath. Would Jacob lose everything he had worked so hard to gain?

Even though angels of God met Jacob at the beginning of his journey, he was "in great fear and distress" (Genesis 32:7). Rightly so! Jacob was at the Lord's mercy as Esau was on his way to see him with four hundred men (Genesis 32:6). As anxiety overtook his soul, he divided those in his care into two groups. If Esau attacked, perhaps he could save half his family.

Jacob prayed, prepared gifts for Esau, and gave his family a plan to follow (Genesis 32). After transporting his family and his fortune safely across the ford of the Jabbok, Jacob retreated back across it to be alone for the night. Was the air still in anticipation of holiness touching earth? There was one more step of preparation to take: a rite of passage. Jacob had wrestled with both Esau and Laban, but a final wrestling match had to take place before he met his brother. Jacob was getting ready to meet his Maker face-to-face (Genesis 32:30).

God, in his great love, wrestled with Jacob, and through that rite of passage new life emerged. Many scholars believe the man Jacob wrestled with was the pre-incarnate Jesus Christ: God in the flesh.

From Genesis 32:22–32, what was new about Jacob after his wrestling match?

_____

_____

_____

_____

## Jacob Walked in a New Way

As the man injured his hip, Jacob was actually healed through this wound. Sometimes our brokenness can bring the greatest blessings. The injury gave him a limp, which means he had to lean—and learn how to walk in a different way. Coming to the end of yourself can be painful, but on the other side is new life as you learn to lean on the Lord as you walk. Our weakness can be our greatest strength when we choose to see it as a doorway to dependence on Jesus (2 Corinthians 12:10–19).

I believe the injury to Jacob's hip was connected to the way he had become too self-reliant—even though God promised that he would not leave him. Think of Jacob's authority figures. His mother told him to deceive his brother, an act that exiled him. His father loved his brother more, and this probably made him feel second-rate. At a young age he had to flee his family, and then he found himself under Laban's selfish leadership. Perhaps Jacob felt he had to rely on himself since the leadership in his life was not trustworthy and at an early age he found himself on his own. With self-reliance comes self-sufficiency and often success. Jacob emerged a savvy businessman surrounded by a large family, persistent in all his endeavors, and always emerging prosperous. I believe God wrestled with him to make him even stronger since the limp left him leaning not on his own strength but on his Lord. Are strength and success bad? No! However, when we begin to place faith in ourselves instead of Jesus, we are on shaky ground.

If your background includes abandonment or unreliable leadership that made you feel you had to rely on yourself and take care of others, then admitting weakness can be scary and unacceptable. But God intended us to find Jesus in our weakness and to rest in his strength! When those in authority over us have abused their power, trusting anyone to take care of us can be frightening. In those situations, self-reliance can emerge. But God is not asking you to trust just anyone—he is asking you to put your trust in him.

Every good builder ensures that a house is built on a solid foundation. Our Dream Builder is an expert, so his dream is built on the foundation of our cornerstone, Jesus Christ (1 Peter 2:4–6; 1 Corinthians 3:9–11; Philippians 3:3–8). Our faith determines our foundation. Our foundation cannot be our talent, our abilities, our wisdom, or our righteousness; it must be Jesus alone.

## Jacob Saw God in a New Way

Jacob was in great distress the night he wrestled with God (Genesis 32:7). God never promised we would be impervious to fear; he promised we could find our comfort in him (John 14:1). If you suffer from anxiety, don't try to bury it.

Because Jacob was injured, he found himself in the arms of a God who loved him beyond his own love for himself. A God who had wisdom beyond Jacob's thinking and resources beyond his wealth. This was a deeper encounter than his experience at Bethel. In the Old Testament, a face-to-face encounter with the Lord was an exceptional experience saved for only a few. What a beautiful truth that in the new covenant of Christ, as daughters of the Dream Builder, we can find a face-to-face connection with God anytime, anywhere!

I love Jacob's attitude at this moment. He cried out saying, "I will not let you go unless you bless me" (Genesis 32:26). When we are experiencing those difficult rites of passage, we need to remember that God is always working on our behalf and wants to bless us (Hebrews 11:6, 12:2).

Even in your failures—especially in your failures—fall into his arms. Jacob deceived Esau but still God protected him. We need Jacob's attitude that says, *I will hang on to my faith that you are for me, God, not against me, and I will not let go of you unless you bless me!* Hosea 12:4 says that Jacob "wept and begged for [the angel's] favor." While wrestling, you may be tempted to question God's goodness. Don't do it! Believe he is *for* you! Otherwise, you may feel unworthy and be tempted to pull back instead of pressing into God. Fight those arrows of doubt with your shield of faith and speak aloud, "I will not let you go unless you bless me!" (Ephesians 6:16).

Press through your doubt and tears and reach out to the One who wants to bring you peace. Press through your past and reach out to the One who wants to redeem you. Press through your fears and take the hand of the One who wants to give you courage to face tomorrow. Press through your failures and reach out to the One who wants to restore you. God is *for* you!

## Jacob Also Had a New Name

God gave Jacob a new name: Israel. The word *name* in this passage can also be translated as "reputation."[1] In other words, God was saying, *I am taking that old label off you, Jacob. You are no longer to be called Jacob, which means "deceiver." You will be called Israel, which means "God prevails," "solider of God," or "he wrestles with God."*[2] *You are no longer a deceiver. You are one who has prevailed with God!*

I find it interesting that God told Jacob about his new name a second time at El Bethel, as we see in Genesis 35:10. God delights in reminding us! We should also continue to remind ourselves of our God-given labels since our negative thoughts, our past, the world, and what others say continue to distract and dissuade us from the truth.

Hallelujah to the God Almighty who desires to peel back those old labels and put his new names on us. Because of Jesus, God always sees me as his "daughter," "ambassador," "beautiful," "worthy," "valuable"; that is my position in Christ. Other people may judge and condemn you, but God sees Jesus in you and calls you by your new names. The law will never change you, but God's new labels will. The more you believe your position in Christ, the more you will change your condition. Behavior always stems from belief.

Second Corinthians 5:17 says, "Therefore, if anyone is in Christ, the new creation has come: The old has gone, the new is here!" Old labels, old habits, old dreams ... God has something greater in store for you. He desires to give you a new name and a new life in Christ—a life that far exceeds your dreams and desires!

## Israel Is Prepared

Jacob was finally ready to face his brother—in humility—because he had new life from leaning on the Lord. As Jacob bowed down, Esau ran and embraced his brother and wept. There was true forgiveness and reconciliation. Healing happened, and now Jacob was ready to go home and God's dream would continue.

All the while Joseph was there with his mother, watching from a distance (Genesis 33:2). I believe Joseph saw how his father's strained hip somehow gave him a new strength. He saw how humility and forgiveness saved his father's life and ultimately his family's life. With this example, God was building his dream. One day Joseph would be like Esau with the power in his hands to harm his family, but Joseph would humble himself and forgive … and in his forgiveness, the dream would continue. The family line of the Messiah would live on.

## Don't Give Up, Give In

After the wrestling ceased, Jacob asked the Lord what his name was and he responded, "Why do you ask my name?" (Genesis 32:29). God did not answer Jacob's question; he simply blessed him. In the wake of wrestling, it's only natural to feel overwhelmed and question God. *Who are you, God? Are you really my protector and redeemer? If you are my healer, why do I hurt?* I believe God questioned Jacob's question because he knew Jacob already knew the answer. Daughter, do not doubt the truth you know. Your Father loves you.

Read the following passage aloud.

> In the womb, that heel, Jacob, got the best of his brother. When he grew up, he tried to get the best of God. But God would not be bested. God bested him. Brought to his knees, Jacob wept and prayed. God found him at Bethel. That's where he spoke with him. God is God-of-the-Angel-Armies, God-Revealed, God-Known. *What are you waiting for? Return to your God! Commit yourself in love, in justice! Wait for your God, and don't give up on him—ever!* (Hosea 12:3–6 MSG, *emphasis mine*)

Daughter of the Dream Builder, what are you waiting for? Has a crisis in your life made you feel as if your life is ending? Don't give up—give in! Return to your Dream Builder. The past is past. Your life is not falling apart … God is getting ready to rebuild it!

## Key Treasure

Our Dream Builder is an expert, so his dream is built on the foundation of our cornerstone, Jesus Christ (1 Peter 2:4–6; 1 Corinthians 3:9–11; Philippians 3:3–8). Our faith determines our foundation. Our foundation cannot be our talent, our abilities, our wisdom, or our righteousness; it must be Jesus alone.

# DAY 5

*For what you have done I will always praise you ... I will hope in your name, for your name is good. —Psalm 52:9*

Like Jacob's wife Rachel, Heather is familiar with the sorrow that settles inside a woman's heart when she cannot conceive a child. For many years, Heather and her husband, Martin, tried but were unable to have a baby. While she will be the first to admit there were difficult days, Heather chose not to become bitter. Instead, she trusted her Dream Builder to build his dream, even if that meant she would not have children of her own.

And then one day a Bethel moment occurred on a still summer night at a Steven Curtis Chapman concert. As Chapman told his story of adopting a child from China, God birthed a dream inside Heather. Heather experienced chills and tears as the crowd around her faded into the background. It was as if she were standing alone before the Lord. Tears were replaced with a wide smile. She could see clearly now. Her descendants would come from China.

When the audience took their seats, Martin turned to Heather and grasped her hand. As he looked into her eyes, they declared simultaneously, "Let's get two!" God had spoken to both of them. Heather was pregnant with a dream from the Dream Builder.

And so Heather and Martin began the lengthy process of adopting a child from China. While waiting, Heather prayed faithfully for God to love and protect her child. In those early stages of her child's life, Heather could not hold her. Half a world away, she could not sing to her, rock her to sleep, or feed her. But just as God promised he would be there with Jacob, he was there with Heather's baby. The Dream Builder had a plan.

Weeks before her trip to China, Heather received information about her baby—the one God had chosen for her to raise. Each word was like a treasure, but perhaps the biggest jewel was the baby's name, Zhi Shua, which means "smart and beautiful."

You see, although Heather could not hold, rock, or swaddle that loved one every day, the baby would hear "you are smart and you are beautiful." It was as if God took Heather's words and carried them across oceans to reach the tender ears of her child through her name.

Eventually, Zhi Shua was secure in her new mother's arms. Heather rocked her and loved her and gave her a new name, Lucie, which means "light." If you meet Lucie, you will quickly see she is every bit as smart and beautiful as her original name proclaimed. Later Heather and Martin went back to China as the Lord led them to adopt a child with special needs they named Phoebe, which means "bright and pure." Phoebe has the most amazing smile. I don't care what kind of day you are having, if she smiles at you, you cannot help but return her grin!

Heather and I have been friends for years now, and I am so excited to have a front-row seat to watch and see God's dream for Lucie and Phoebe bring his light and love into the world in a special way.

## The Significance of Names

Names are important. In the Bible, the Lord sometimes changed people's names after life-changing events. Abram became Abraham. Sarai became Sarah. Jacob became Israel. Simon became Peter. Saul became Paul.

Last week we also saw how the names Jacob assigned to places reflected or symbolized the experience he had with the Lord.

*Bethel* was the name Jacob gave to that special place where God revealed himself in a dream and also spoke to Jacob. Years later God called Jacob to return to Bethel with his entire family, including Joseph. After that second experience, Jacob changed the name to *El Bethel*. *Bethel* means "the house of God," but *El Bethel* means "the God of the house of God."

Jon Courson writes this in his commentary:

> This shows monumental maturity, for Jacob understands that it's not the house of God that is important, but the God who dwells therein. So, too, it's not worship that's important, but the God whom we worship. It's not the Bible that's important, but the God of the Bible. You see, the Word is not an end in itself. The goal of Bible study is not to try and gain more intellectual or theological understanding. It's more than that. The Word of God is simply a door I go through many times a day to meet the God of the Word.[3]

## God's Names Illuminate His Character

God has numerous names that illuminate and reveal many facets of who he is. Here are five names of God found in the Bible. Circle the one that is most meaningful to you at this time in your life and briefly explain why.

The LORD Will Provide (Genesis 22:14)

The LORD Is My Banner (Exodus 17:15)

The LORD Is Peace (Judges 6:24)

The LORD Is My Shepherd (Psalm 23)

The LORD Who Heals You (Exodus 15:26)

_____

_____

_____

_____

Provider. Protector. Peace. Shepherd. Healer ... and so much more. Read the following aloud.

*Lord, you are my provider when I am in want. You are my love and protection in the face of rejection. You are my peace in the storm and my shepherd to guide my steps. You are the healer of my broken heart.*

The patriarchs "called on the name of the LORD" (Genesis 13:4; 21:33; 26:25). God's names are more than identification—they are revelations of his promises to you as his child. This is why one of your IMPACT questions includes finding an image of God to *trust*.

You may know that God is a provider, but do you trust he is your own *personal* provider? Not just for the people in the Bible, or your pastor, or your small group leader, but for you personally. Make him personal in your life by trusting that God is who he says he is in the Bible as you reach out to him in prayer using one of his many names. Worship is another way to build your trust in our Almighty God.

Read Romans 1:21–25 and Genesis 35.

Why do you think God asked Jacob and his family to surrender their idols before they built their altar?

_____

_____

_____

Why is it vital that we know and believe the truth of God as revealed to us through his Word, and not simply through our circumstances or our thinking?

_____

_____

_____

How do you think worship loosens our grip on the idols that can creep into our hearts?

_____

_____

The Dream Builder's dreams are God-sized. Idols simply do not have the ability to bring our dreams to pass. When God reigns in the heart of a woman, his glory will illuminate the path of her purpose and she is free to step into the spacious place of the God-given dream that has already been planned for her (Romans 12:2; Psalm 16:5–7; Jeremiah 29:11; Ephesians 2:10).

Worship makes God bigger, and our idols simply lose their luster. Worship promotes truth over lies in our minds and builds an altar to God in our hearts, where we can sacrifice the things that hold us back from him.

You serve an almighty, powerful God who is able to do the amazing in your life when you place your trust in him. Call upon the name of the Lord and worship him. Reflect, speak, sing, or pray! Build a throne in your heart for God and his glory as you worship his name. God has great things in store for you—oh, worship his holy name!

## Key Treasure

The Dream Builder's dreams are God-sized. Idols simply do not have the ability to bring our dreams to pass. When God reigns in the heart of a woman, his glory will illuminate the path of her purpose and she is free to step into the spacious place of the God-given dream that has already been planned for her.

# DAY 6

"Yet to all who did receive him, to those who believed in his name, he gave the right to become children of God—*children born not of natural descent, nor of human decision or a husband's will, but born of God.*" —*John 1:12–13, emphasis mine*

Becoming a daughter of the Dream Builder brings a whole new world to light. We have uncovered some marvelous truths sprinkled throughout this chapter about the blessings available to every child of God. Along the way you may have asked this question:

*How do I become a daughter of the Dream Builder?*

For Joseph, and for you today, becoming a child of God has been and always will be about faith through calling on the name of the Lord. It was about faith from the very beginning. "Abram believed the LORD, and he credited it to him as righteousness" (Genesis 15:6). Abraham gained righteousness by believing God would indeed do what he had said and make him into a great nation—not through his good works but through his faith (Galatians 3:6–9).

Nicodemus, a Pharisee and member of the Jewish ruling council, wrestled with this question. He considered his life. He was very religious, had extensive knowledge of the Scriptures, and was also wealthy and well respected. He had status and security, yet he still had questions.

Who was Jesus? This humble man whose hands brought healing and whose words brought life also taught things that threatened Nicodemus's status as a Pharisee. The tension in his heart was too much to ignore. Nicodemus had to learn the truth. In the still of the night, he slipped away secretly to find answers. A budding faith hastened his footsteps. Leaving the traditions of his forefathers, risking the ridicule of his family and fellow Pharisees, he found Jesus.

John 3:1–18 records their meeting. Pretend you are Nicodemus discovering how to become a child of the Dream Builder for the first time.

From verses 5–8 and 16–18, how does one become "born again"?

-------------------------------------------------

-------------------------------------------------

-------------------------------------------------

-------------------------------------------------

## Just Believe

Simply believe. It was too easy! *I don't have to achieve it … just believe it? This can't be!* The hundreds of laws that were such a heavy load on Nicodemus's back had been a way of life for generations in his family. Righteousness was earned through keeping the law. Just believe?

Whether you have attended church for years or are a professing atheist, becoming a child of God is the same. It's not something you achieve—it's something you receive through what you believe.

> If you declare with your mouth, "Jesus is Lord," and believe in your heart that God raised him from the dead, you will be saved. For it is with your heart that you believe and are justified, and it is with your mouth that you profess your faith and are saved. As Scripture says, "Anyone who believes in him will never be put to shame." For there is no difference between Jew and Gentile—the same Lord is Lord of all and richly blesses all who call on him, for, "Everyone who calls on the name of the Lord will be saved." (Romans 10:9–13)

"Everyone who calls on the name of the LORD will be saved" (Joel 2:32). You don't have to live perfectly. It's not about attending church every Sunday or Bible study every week. Salvation is not something you earn—it's a gift from God you receive by believing.

Because God loves you and knows you could never live perfectly, he sent his Son, Jesus, who was perfect, to die on the cross, paying the penalty for your sin. By calling on his name, you can be forgiven and set free to live for him.

Our old nature causes us to sin (meaning to miss the mark of God's perfection). The Bible clearly says we have all sinned (Romans 3:23). Instead of trusting in our own efforts, we can put our trust in the sacrifice Christ made on the cross by calling on his name for forgiveness. God is righteous, and eternity with him is true life and righteousness. We cannot join him, though, in our sinfulness. Our sin estranges us from God, and eternal separation from the God of life and love is death.

God knew we could not save ourselves from sin. If we could, we could claim our own righteousness and Christ would have died in vain. The law does not provide the solution. We can only become a child of God through his grace (unearned favor). The law made it clear we could never live perfect lives and showed us our need for a Savior. God sent his only Son to redeem us (John 3:16).

In his great love, the Creator of the universe sent his Son to die in our place. Jesus paid the supreme price for our sin. He laid his life down for us. *It is because God wants us to live for him that shame and guilt were taken away on the cross.* It was because of his love for us that Jesus went to the cross so you and I could have a personal relationship with him and become his child, born again into a new family. Our sin has been nailed to the cross.

The power of sin was broken when God raised Jesus to life, triumphant over death! The curse of sin was "reversed" and all of creation was freed from the bonds of death through Jesus' victory. We all have the opportunity to receive that freedom, to take part in his victory. What an immeasurable blessing!

Salvation is a gift. Jesus has done his part on the cross, but we must receive his gift by faith (Ephesians 2:8). How do we do this? The Bible says when we confess with our mouths and believe in our hearts that Jesus is Lord, we are saved from the penalty and power of sin (Romans 10:8–13).

## Are You a Child of God?

Are you in the family of God? Perhaps you are like Nicodemus: confused but wanting answers in your life. Maybe this move requires a huge leap of faith into a brand-new way of thinking. Don't place your faith in your traditions or your feelings or your family—walk by faith in God. Wherever you are in your life, know that Jesus stands with his arms open wide, ready to adopt you as his child (Ephesians 1:5). All you have to do is call on his name.

What are you waiting for? An abundant life awaits you on the other side!

Let's call on the Lord in prayer and receive the Father's love. If you are not yet a Christian, make that choice right now. Choose forgiveness, choose freedom, choose life—choose Jesus. If you are a Christian, may this prayer remind you of your position in Christ!

Climb up into your Father's lap. He is waiting to set you free. Please pray with me.

> *Father, I call upon your name! You are my Savior. Thank you for sending Jesus to die in my place and bring me into new life through his resurrection. Your grace cleanses me completely and continually from my mistakes. Your grace is so vast I cannot understand it in my own mind. And so I come before you in simple trust to let go of my shame. I joyfully acknowledge that I cannot earn my salvation in my own ability. I acknowledge that the power of sin is taken away only by your grace, your favor that I don't deserve and could never earn. I choose to believe you today and trust in the supernatural strength of the Holy Spirit.*
>
> *Thank you, Jesus, for taking all my shame. I lay it at your cross. Thank you, Jesus, for paying the penalty for all my sins—past, present, and future. I lay them at the cross. I confess you are my Lord and Savior. Thank you for raising me, spotless, to life with you! I thank you that I don't have to hide anymore. Because I am your child now, I will run to you for help instead of hiding. You have a dream for me—a destiny designed to help others, and I am ready to follow. You paid it all for me, and I give my life to you. AMEN!*

# VIDEO SESSION NOTES

Session 2
## CALL ON HIS NAME
*Genesis 35:1-15*

# Chapter 3
# HIS TREASURE

# DAY 1
## Nourish Scripture: Genesis 37

### 1 PRAY.

Begin your time with God in prayer.

### 2 MEDITATE ON GOD'S WORD.

Using your Anchor of Truth Card* from last week's Nourish Notes, renew your mind on that truth. Quiet and focus your thoughts. Pray the truth. Say the truth. Meditate on God's truth.

### 3 TAKE THE *REVEAL* STEP OF THE NOURISH BIBLE STUDY METHOD.

Connect with Jesus by studying the Weekly Nourish Scripture and allowing the Holy Spirit to reveal truth in those verses. Prayerfully read over and reflect on the passage. Mark any phrases, verses, or words that catch your attention. Journal and learn as the Lord leads you.

---

*Anchor of Truth Cards are available at www.TreasuredMinistries.com/shop

# DAY 2
### Nourish Scripture: Genesis 37

**1  PRAY.**
Begin your time with God in prayer.

**2  MEDITATE ON GOD'S WORD.**
Using your Anchor of Truth Card* from last week's Nourish Notes, renew your mind on that truth. Quiet and focus your thoughts. Pray the truth. Say the truth. Meditate on God's truth.

**3  TAKE THE *RESPOND* STEP OF THE NOURISH BIBLE STUDY METHOD.**
Respond to activate truth in your life. The acronym **IMPACT** provides questions to help you apply the truth from your weekly Nourish Scripture. **Sometimes you may not have answers for all six questions.**

**IMAGE OF GOD TO TRUST?** An attribute of God, Jesus, or the Holy Spirit to trust.

**MESSAGE TO SHARE?** A word of encouragement, truth, or prayer to share.

**PROMISE TO TREASURE?** A promise in the Bible to believe.

**ACTION TO TAKE?** A specific step God is calling you to take.

**CORE IDENTITY IN CHRIST TO AFFIRM?** A truth about how God sees you to affirm.

**TRANSGRESSION TO CONFESS?** A sin to acknowledge for help, healing, and restoration through Christ.

*Anchor of Truth Cards are available at www.TreasuredMinistries.com/shop

# DAY 3

Nourish Scripture: Genesis 37

**1 PRAY.**

Begin your time with God in prayer.

**2 MEDITATE ON GOD'S WORD.**

Using your Anchor of Truth Card* from last week's Nourish Notes, renew your mind on that truth. Quiet and focus your thoughts. Pray the truth. Say the truth. Meditate on God's truth.

**3 TAKE THE *RENEW* STEP OF THE NOURISH BIBLE STUDY METHOD.**

Like an anchor that secures its vessel, biblical meditation secures truth to transform your life. Take five minutes to *renew* your mind by focusing on one word, verse, or truth that the Holy Spirit revealed through the Bible during your week of study. Record your truth below and on your Anchor of Truth card.* Quiet your thoughts. Focus on the truth. Read the truth. Pray the truth.

**4 UTILIZE YOUR *ANCHOR OF TRUTH* CARD AS A BOOKMARK TO CULTIVATE A DAILY PRACTICE OF BIBLICAL MEDITATION.**

Place your Anchor of Truth Card* in your Bible study workbook to bookmark tomorrow's day of study. Let your Anchor of Truth bookmark remind you to pause and renew your mind on God's Word. Repeat this process daily, continuing to reflect on your Anchor of Truth to start your quiet time until the next week, when God reveals another truth to you.

*Anchor of Truth Cards are available at www.TreasuredMinistries.com/shop

# DAY 4

Unless the LORD builds the house, the builders labor in vain.
—*Psalm 127:1*

*The Dream Builder stood before his daughter and smiled broadly at his beautiful creation. "My daughter, you were built to bring meaning to this world. Do you want to use all I have provided for you . . . to live life to the fullest?"*

*He carefully cast this question, longing for her to see what he saw—a valuable treasure gifted to change the world. Would she be brave enough to believe that she was a masterpiece fashioned for a specific purpose?*

*Would she listen to the Dream Builder? Or would she continue to listen to the tempter's taunts. His accusations. His lies that she was worthless. Unable. Inadequate.*

*The Dream Builder paused. He loved her and would not give up. He would continue to remind her that she, just as she was, could make a difference. He would continue until she believed. Until she grasped the dream he had for her. Until she moved ahead knowing that with his plan and provision, his dream for her life would come to pass.*

*His eyes sparkled and he laughed with joy as he pondered the richness of his plan for her. For this generation, she was created. For this generation, her life was given to be a gift to others. Maybe today would be the day she would finally believe she was created to live for his glory.*

The Lord who built the mountains with all their majesty is the one who created you to reflect his glory and bring meaning to this world (Genesis 1:27; Psalm 139:14).

I was built to bring meaning to this world . . . and so were you.

## The Dream Builder Created Joseph to Fulfill His Dream

The Dream Builder carefully crafted Joseph to accomplish his purpose. His character and his calling were chosen with care. A famine on the horizon threatened the existence of God's chosen people, the bloodline that would eventually bring the Messiah. God would use Joseph to intercept hunger and save the lives of many, physically and spiritually, for generations to come.

In the stillness of the night, God planted a seed of his plan for Joseph's life through two dreams. Describe Joseph's two dreams (Genesis 37:1–11). If you were asked to interpret each dream, what are some thoughts you might have?

The sheaves of wheat:

_____

_____

_____

The sun and stars:

_____

_____

_____

Joseph was only seventeen, but his dreams revealed a destiny of leadership. The sheaves represented the world's resources, and the stars symbolized the world's rulers. The picture projected not only leadership over his family but also world leadership with vast resources at his disposal.

## Part of God's Provision: Personality and Character

From your reading this week in Genesis 37, which of Joseph's characteristics and personality traits were tools that would make him a good leader?

_____

_____

_____

Read Acts 7:9–10. From verse 10, what did the Dream Builder build in Joseph to provide for his vision?

_____

_____

_____

Integrity, courage, and confidence were three strands tightly woven into the fabric of Joseph's personality. He *confidently* believed in the dream and *boldly* shared his dream with his family.

Joseph's *integrity* would not allow him to ignore his brothers' wrong behavior. Although the Bible does not tell us exactly what his brothers did, it must have been something that affected the family because their actions compelled Joseph to tell his father.

When his brothers betrayed Joseph and left him in a pit, I believe his courage strengthened him and carried him through the circumstances.

God instilled incredible *insight* and *wisdom* in Joseph's mind. He could interpret dreams and thus see into the future. In the future, this gift would exalt him in the eyes of Pharaoh of Egypt. When Joseph was promoted to a position for God's purposes, God gave him the insight and wisdom—and a plan—to save the lives of many. Not only the lives of the Egyptians, but also the lives of God's chosen people.

God's hand was on Joseph's life—and his hand is on yours.

## The Dream Builder Has Provided for You Too

Like Joseph, the way you are wired—your personality and passions, your character and natural abilities, and your spiritual gifts—are part of the provision for your God-given vision. The Dream Builder has equipped you with just the right tools you need to build your dream. He fashioned you to fuel your future.

Not only were you wired for his wonderful work at birth, but the Dream Builder also imparted spiritual gifts to you the moment you were born into God's family. Read 1 Corinthians 12:4–11 and Romans 12:3–8.

According to 1 Corinthians 12:11 and Romans 12:3, who determines what spiritual gifts are given?

According to 1 Corinthians 12:4–7, what are our spiritual gifts to be used for?

If you were responsible for giving Joseph the tools he needed to fulfill his dream, which spiritual gifts would you choose and why?

What spiritual gifts do you think the Dream Builder has given you?

## Discover Your Gifts

God's provision, including our spiritual gifts, flows to us and through us for his glory and the good of others. The Dream Builder determines how we are created and what spiritual gifts will flow in our lives.

When we recognize how we are wired, we can focus on our core strengths and grow in the gifts the Lord has given us. God will bring others into our lives who are gifted in areas we are not. Working together, each of us contributing what God has provided for us, we can bring God's life-changing love to the world.

## God's Temples: The Building and Believers

Generations after Joseph lived, a leader among God's chosen people named Solomon would ask the Dream Builder for the gift of wisdom. King Solomon made his mark on Israel's history by building the temple in Jerusalem. His Spirit-infused wisdom can be seen in Proverbs and Ecclesiastes. Solomon also wrote Psalm 127. Recite Psalm 127:1–2 to yourself.

> Unless the LORD builds the house, the builders labor in vain. Unless the LORD watches over the city, the watchmen stand guard in vain. In vain you rise early and stay up late, toiling for food to eat—for he grants sleep to those he loves. (Psalm 127:1–2)

The temple in Jerusalem was built according to the Dream Builder's plan, down to the last detail. As Solomon finished the last stroke according to God's design, he declared, "I have indeed built a magnificent temple for you, a place for you to dwell forever" (1 Kings 8:13). While the temple was magnificent and built to the Lord's specifications, there was a greater temple yet to come.

> Don't you know that you yourselves are God's temple and that God's Spirit dwells in your midst? (1 Corinthians 3:16)

You are that greater temple. Like Solomon's temple, you are built with splendor, precisely to God's plan. You are God's treasure, designed for a unique purpose (Deuteronomy 7:6; Ephesians 2:10). You are beautiful. God made all creation good (Genesis 1:31). You are part of his creation. You are fitted for a purpose. You have everything you need for what God has called you to do.

## Celebrate the Way the Dream Builder Created You

> When you strive to be someone you are not, you are laboring in vain. Frustration and a sense of failure will find you. Have you ever experienced a sense of frustration or failure because you compared yourself with another woman or tried to be someone other than the person God created you to be?

---

---

---

Accepting the way God designed and gifted you allows him to build your house, to plant the dream of your God-designed purpose in your heart, and to help you use your gifts to fulfill that dream. Comparing yourself to others and their gifts is a waste of time and energy. Mourning over what you are not is refusing to accept—in gratitude—the gifts God has given you. And thinking you are better than anyone else because of the way God made you and gifted you is pride. God gives each of his daughters what she needs to accomplish his purpose. You are anointed for YOUR God-given dream, not someone else's purpose.

You can experience security, rest, and peace when you believe the Dream Builder built you specifically and perfectly to accomplish his purpose for your life. You are a unique creation designed for a specific dream the Lord has built for you.

*She took a good hard look at the Dream Builder. He was giving her permission to rest in how she was created—and she was relieved. She could stop pretending to be someone she was not. She decided to stop comparing herself with other women and find value by celebrating how the Dream Builder created her. She wanted God to use her life for others. And then it dawned on her. He did have a plan and a purpose for her life. And he would provide all she needed to accomplish that purpose. She would simply need to believe, rest, and allow God to build his dream through her.*

*She squared her shoulders, sat up straight, and opened her mouth. "I am a magnificent masterpiece built for God's glory. I have all the tools I need to build his dream in my life. I am not a mistake. I am lacking nothing. I am his treasure designed for a unique purpose." She smiled.*

Rest in how the Lord built you. You were meant to shine.

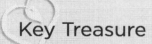

## Key Treasure

You can experience security, rest, and peace when you believe the Dream Builder built you specifically and perfectly to accomplish his purpose for your life. You are a unique creation designed for a specific dream the Lord has built for you.

# DAY 5

Unless the LORD watches over the city, the guards stand watch in vain.
*—Psalm 127:1*

*The Dream Builder's words filled her with confidence. Like fresh wind filling the sails of a boat, her new thoughts about herself and the Dream Builder gave her energy to move forward. She took her hands off the rudder and began charting her course according to the Creator's plan. She believed she was built for a purpose, and this gave her a daring boldness and urgency for her journey. As excitement escalated in her heart, she called out to friends and family standing on the nearby shore to tell them of the amazing dream.*

*She knew she was God's treasure, divinely created for a unique purpose. Did they see it too?*

*Many cheered her on, as they were also walking in their purpose. Although their dreams were different, they could celebrate alongside her. They remembered the day they had realized they were built to bring God glory—and so they understood her newly found joy and freedom. Some even marveled at how their gifts and dreams worked with hers to carry out God's plan as they all sailed on with the same destination in mind: bringing God's love to this world.*

*But there were others who would not return her smile. Envy wound its way into their hearts like overgrown poison ivy and suffocated love. Although the Dream Builder had built them beautifully and provided them with all they needed to fulfill their God-given dreams, they coveted her gifts. Malice and hatred quickly followed, and they began to throw stones through her sails.*

*There were others she cared about who, instead of rejoicing with her and encouraging her, flooded her with well-meaning warnings. "What you are trying to do is impossible." "You can't do that—don't set yourself up for a fall!" "Don't you see the risk? Stay where you are safe!" Sometimes these cautions were motivated by genuine concern. Sometimes they were stirred up by envy or jealousy. But every time, they made her hesitate. Could God build his dream through her?*

*Her confidence turned to confusion. Her passion and determination to follow the Dream Builder began to crumble. She tried again to focus on what the Dream Builder had told her, but the other voices seemed louder. Her double-mindedness diffused the wind from her sails, and she was tossed about in the waves—directionless. Suddenly a storm surged. Unable to steer because of her tattered sails, she was carried away to a foreign land. Surrounded by waters on a deserted island, she began to question what the Dream Builder had told her.*

*Although she could not see him or feel his presence, the Dream Builder was still there. He would guard her and his dream. He would rescue her.*

## Envy and Jealousy: Roadblocks to Fulfilling Our God-Given Dreams

When others are envious or jealous of what God is doing in our lives, of the gifts he has given us, their attitudes and words can confuse and discourage us. When we focus on what others think instead of our Creator and his plan and provision for us, we can lose our passion. We can find ourselves on detours or even facing a roadblock to doing what God has called us to do.

A similar pitfall arises when we act on the envy or jealousy we feel toward others. When this happens, we lose sight of God's plan for us and focus on what others have instead of cultivating the dream God has given us.

Envy and jealousy are fleshly feelings that can dominate our thinking, distort our reality, and push us to actions we did not know we could take. Like a tornado, they can carry our thoughts, and therefore our actions, in a wrong direction.

## Jealousy and Envy in Joseph's Story

Seeds of envy sown in the hearts of Joseph's brothers gave way to hate and malice, and they hurled our hero into a deep pit. Describe some of the reasons the brothers were envious of Joseph.

Do you think they had a right to feel the way they did? Why or why not?

When the brothers acted on their envy, destruction followed. List some negative results of their jealousy.

I imagine if I had been one of Joseph's brothers, I would have been envious also. Bestowing that beautiful coat of colors on his beloved Joseph, Jacob didn't even try to hide his favoritism. Perhaps you too know what it feels like to be the one who is not the favorite. Being loved and valued is a core heart need. I understand why the brothers felt the way they did.

Joseph's bold announcement of his dream seemed to be the straw that broke the camel's back. The brothers lost control over their emotions and began to make choices based on their feelings, without any remorse. But envy lied to them. Their choice to satisfy their feelings did not change their father's devotion, nor would it prevent Joseph's dream from moving on.

Joseph's brothers not only reaped destruction but also missed their own blessing. Throwing Joseph into a pit did not make their father love them more—it only caused him to be overcome with grief. Their attempts to get rid of Joseph did not stop him from becoming a world leader. Every day the brothers bore the guilt of their actions as they watched their father immersed in grief. Can you imagine the weight of living with that lie lingering like a dark storm cloud? Imagine all they missed by not supporting Joseph. What an exciting adventure they could have had walking with Joseph and helping him instead of hindering the dream.

I believe Joseph's brothers deep down desired acceptance and significance. Their envy of Joseph went far beyond a coat of many colors or a dream. The truth was that they were already significant and accepted—by God's design. They were also God's chosen treasure (Deuteronomy 7:6). He had dreams for them, but they were different from his dreams for Joseph. Although Jacob was not devoted equally to his sons, God loved each of the twelve brothers with unconditional, deep, everlasting—and equal—love.

The brothers' desire to gain love and acceptance was not wrong. But trying to get that need met apart from God caused trouble.

## Recognize That Envy and Jealousy Are Destructive

What do you learn about jealousy and envy from the following scriptures?

Proverbs 14:30

_____

_____

_____

Galatians 5:19–21

_____

_____

_____

James 4:1–3

_____

_____

_____

You may feel as if you have a right to be jealous or envious of someone else. And if you told me your story, I might agree with you—I have been there myself. But acting on jealousy and envy never brings positive results for anyone.

The enemy can capitalize on jealousy and envy to carry out his schemes. Jealousy and envy steal your peace of mind and prevent you from walking in the Spirit. When you give in to these emotions, you sow destructive seeds into your life. Your flesh desires what is contrary to the Spirit. Don't be deceived. Sowing into jealousy and envy brings a harvest of destruction (Galatians 6:7).

## Only Christ Can Free You

When an emotion like envy outweighs the truth in God's Word, and we base our decisions and our actions on our feelings, we are yielding to the wrong leader. We should never put our emotions in the driver's seat of our decisions, which can bring commotion in our life. When we are led by the Spirit, he brings us into the abundant life.

When you have feelings that go against your faith, the most powerful thing you can do is take them to God. Don't suppress your feelings—or feel condemned by them. Take them to Jesus in prayer by expressing your emotions to him and ask him to show you the truth through his Word (Hebrews 2:14–18; 4:12–16).

The truth is that God has already established his dream for your life, and he will give you everything you need to accomplish that purpose (Ephesians 2:10; Philippians 4:19). As God's child, you have a specific purpose that can only be given and designed by your heavenly Father. God is the potter and we are the clay (Jeremiah 29:11; Isaiah 64:8). You can only be you. Every God-given task is great in God's eyes (Matthew 18:2; Romans 12:4–6). Your value and God's love for you are not determined by what you do but in the fact that you are his child! The more you help others grow in their purpose, the more you will find yours (Galatians 6:7). When you accept these truths, they will inspire you to connect, not compete, with your sisters in Christ.

## Turn Your Faith Back to God Through Praise and Prayer

As you come to Jesus, bring your desires to God and trust in his perfect provision for your life (1 Peter 5:7; Philippians 4:19; Matthew 9–11). Be honest with God about the desires in your heart and he will give you his perspective (James 4:1–3). Seek God first in all things and trust him in his love for you to give you what you need (Matthew 6:33).

As you pray, remember that praise and thanksgiving are God's prescription to help highlight God's personal provision in your life. Reflect on his blessings in your life and you'll find yourself turning your eyes to your Father. Praise allows you to see how God is blessing you in his perfect way. God is a giver, and he does not withhold any good thing from his children (Luke 11:10–12; James 1:17). If you ask for something and don't receive it, rest in God's perfect plan. He knows what is best.

If you like, pause to pray. Go to Jesus and share your heart with the Father. Be honest with your Dream Builder. Cry in his lap if you need to. God loves you and does not condemn you, but stands with arms open ready to help you (Romans 8:14). Declare your trust in him again even when you don't understand (Proverbs 3:5–6).

## God Builds the House—and Then Guards the City

Let's go back to Solomon's psalm and soak up some truth. Read the scripture again.

> Unless the LORD builds the house, the builders labor in vain. Unless the LORD watches over the city, the guards stand watch in vain. (Psalm 127:1)

God not only builds the house, but he guards the city. He will not build a dream in your heart and then leave you to pursue it alone. God does not promise to guard our agendas, but he will always guard his dream.

But what if you are the object of someone else's jealousy and envy and, like Joseph, find yourself in a pit? Has God stopped guarding you? Absolutely not! (See Psalm 23:4.)

The pit did not prevent Joseph's dream from becoming a reality—God was with Joseph. God continued to guard the dream because it was his plan to accomplish his purpose.

God turned Joseph's pit tragedy into a treasure. God can guard you from the pit, but if you find yourself in one, rest assured there is purpose in the pit (Psalm 40:2; Romans 8:28). Jesus was betrayed for money, stripped of his robe, and crucified on the cross. But God turned tragedy into treasure. He offered us a gift of love so great it is almost beyond our comprehension. And he was glorified.

Joseph also was sold for money. He was stripped of his robe and his dignity. God used the betrayal of Judas to fulfill his plan for Jesus. And God used the betrayal of Joseph's brothers to fulfill his plan for Joseph and all God's chosen people. Similarly, no evil can come against you that God cannot turn around for his glory (Isaiah 54:17; Romans 8:28).

The pit put necessary boundaries in place for Joseph to be away from his family. His brothers hated him and could have potentially killed him if he had stayed around, because they had not dealt with their jealousy and envy. Joseph also needed to be away from his doting father to learn dependence on God. Because Jacob was so attentive to Joseph, the young man may not have been motivated to lean on the Dream Builder. Sometimes we have to be pushed out of the nest, pruned, and even allowed to spend time in the pit to learn we can fly on the wings of the Holy Spirit (John 15:2).

The pit also moved Joseph to a place where he would receive the provision necessary for his dream. At that time, Egypt led the world in knowledge, medicine, and wealth. However, Egypt was a destination Joseph probably would have avoided because God had called his chosen people to Canaan. Also, Egypt was a reminder of negative history in Joseph's family. Abraham had previously made two trips to Egypt, each time making poor choices that resulted in negative consequences (Genesis 12:10; 20:2). But the pit forced Joseph to move to Egypt, the place he needed to be.

God's ways are so different from ours (Isaiah 55:8–9). Perhaps you don't understand why you are in a particular place or situation—but God does! And he has a plan. If you have been rejected, shake the dust off your feet and trust that God is planting you somewhere you can bloom (Matthew 10:14).

The pit also built in Joseph character that was necessary to make him a great leader. It helped him learn humility, a quality vital for godly leadership (Philippians 2:3). When we are hard-pressed, God can use our experience to mold us to be more like his Son (Romans 8:28–29).

Delight in your dry cistern, believing there is a purpose in the pit! Declare your dependence on God and know he will rescue you. Whatever you do, hold on to your faith and never doubt God's love or his dream for you.

## No Pit Can Keep You from God's Purpose

Daughters of the Dream Builder, beware of jealousy and envy. Christ alone can free us from those negative emotions. Dispel those feelings with the truth in God's Word. Turn your faith back to God to build and guard his dream. And if you find yourself in the pit, rejoice knowing there is purpose in the pit!

Above all, realize that Satan is the real enemy behind all hate and jealousy. The enemy is the one who comes to kill, steal, and destroy (John 10:10).

However, the Dream Builder is guarding you with a watchful eye. Nothing that comes against you will overtake you (Romans 8:31–32). There is no pit that can keep you from God's purpose. The Dream Builder builds the dream, and he guards it for you.

*The tears fell from her eyes and saturated the sand where they fell. Her torn sail could no longer carry her to her destination. Surrounded by water on every side, she felt trapped, as if she were in a deep pit with no way to escape.*

*She felt a strong, rugged hand on her shoulder. It was the Dream Builder. As she looked up, he extended his hand to help her to her feet.*

*"I don't understand," she whispered. He smiled and held her face. Then he placed a brass shovel in her hands. Her eyes questioned the Dream Builder. Why the shovel?*

*"Dig, my child." And as she sank the shovel into the sand of that deserted island, she found treasure beneath the surface. She continued to dig. The treasure, sparkling in the sun, was endless. Her tears turned to joy. She clapped and hugged the Dream Builder with delight. There on the island was the provision she needed.*

*A rich laugh echoed from the Dream Builder as he watched his daughter pursue his purpose for her with passion. He was filled with joy as she unearthed the treasures from her tragedy.*

*"My daughter, I chose you. I built you. I will guard you and the dream I have given you, for it is my dream that you may bring my love to others. The weapons of hate formed against you with jealousy and envy will never prosper—they will only bring you into your purpose. This is your heritage" (see Isaiah 54:17).*

## Key Treasure

Your value and God's love for you are not determined by what you do but in the fact that you are his child! The more you help others grow in their purpose, the more you will find yours (Galatians 6:7). When you accept these truths, they will inspire you to connect, not compete, with your sisters in Christ.

# DAY 6

In vain you rise early and stay up late, toiling for food to eat—
for he grants sleep to those he loves. *—Psalm 127:2*

*"They were wrong about me! I do have purpose! I am valuable and loveable. Look at the treasure the Dream Builder has given me."*

*As she began to serve him, another force rose up in her and pushed her to focus on herself. She could not let go of the words flowing from those who had thrown stones in her sails. She wanted to prove to them that she was valuable. She wanted to hear from them that she was significant. Inside, she feared they were right about her. And so she set out to prove to them, and herself, that she was acceptable and valuable.*

*She worked hard, terrified of failing. She rose early and stayed up late, toiling and toiling until she was exhausted and weary. But no matter how hard she worked, she never felt it was enough. And so she worked harder and harder—and eventually she lost her joy.*

*The Dream Builder stood by and sighed. He already loved her and had told her she was valuable. He was sad to see her striving in her own strength in this endless, meaningless pursuit, looking to others to determine her value. She was working hard to gain something she already had. While she engaged in this meaningless toil, she was missing the amazing life he had planned for her.*

Every day when you wake up in the morning, you have to decide what voices you will listen to that day. Whose words will determine your worth? You are God's chosen treasure, designed for a unique purpose. Freedom comes when you daily embrace this truth for yourself.

## My Search for Significance

When I was young, my heart was deeply wounded. To handle that hurt, I set out on a pursuit of performance. I was determined to be significant in all the ways that matter to this world. I felt so bad about myself I wanted to prove that I was good. I worked very hard, driving myself to perform. Achievement was my antidote for how awful I felt about myself on the inside.

On the outside, I may have appeared to be serving others, but I was really serving myself and my need for others to think well of me. Terrified of failing, I would do whatever it took to be the best. Feeling significant was as essential as food for me. Those words of Solomon were so true of me: "In vain you rise early and stay up late, toiling for food to eat" (Psalm 127:2).

When I began to believe my value was not based on what others thought about me, God began a healing process. After a sifting season that sent rains to wash away sand covering my rock, I began to learn to draw my value from God (Luke 6:47–49). The result was not only rest in my soul but also a release to love others in greater measure. When you start believing a person's value is based on the fact that they are created in God's image, you too will be released to love them more.

## Joseph Didn't Find Significance Through Others— and Neither Will You

Are you looking for your significance through the eyes of others? When you look to other people to draw your value—you will find yourself on an endless, meaningless quest.

Joseph's brothers, full of envy, could not validate Joseph—or his dream. When Joseph made a bold move describing his dream to his brothers, I believe he was confident. I believe he had a strong faith in God and was excited about his dream. But I also believe he hoped his bold announcement would prove to his brothers that he was valuable and significant. *Look, brothers! Your hateful words were wrong about me. God thinks I am special. One day you will bow down to me. I am important—you were wrong.*

In contrast to Joseph's brothers, his father, Jacob, loved him deeply. Because Joseph was the favorite, I found his father's reaction to the dream fascinating. He did not validate Joseph—he rebuked him! Was there a part of Jacob that was afraid to let go of his beloved son? Would Joseph need him anymore? Was he afraid his son would fail? Was he disappointed in Joseph's poor judgment in parading God's plan before his brothers, who hated him?

Whatever the reason, when Joseph proclaimed God's purpose for his life, neither his brothers, who detested him, nor his father, who adored him, validated his dream.

## Allow Your Dream Builder to Determine Your Value

The Dream Builder builds the dreamer and the dream. Other people cannot give you value. This must come from the Dream Builder.

*You are his treasure designed for a unique purpose.*

What people in your life are like Joseph's brothers? So insecure in themselves that they cannot speak kind words to you. If you look to them for value, you will always leave their presence feeling "less than."

Trying to prove to those who envy you that you are valuable is a losing battle. You cannot stop them from being jealous of you. That is their choice. But you can choose what voice you will listen to.

What about the "Jacobs"—those people in our lives who love and give to us in amazing ways, as Jacob loved his son?

Others may love us greatly, but we cannot expect them to validate our worth. That is an unrealistic expectation that puts a severe strain on any relationship. Don't look to them. Don't even look to your achievements. Look to the Dream Builder.

## Serving *for* Significance—or from a Place of God's Significance

The dreams God plants in our hearts are motivated by his love for us and for others. He gifts us to share his love with others. If we ever start using those gifts for our own glory instead of his, we are treading on dangerous ground. While this self-centered kind of service can be carefully contained within the walls of religion, only when we allow the Lord to break us free of self and start living for Christ will we begin to truly love others.

God does not provide you with gifts and tools to build your kingdom for your validation; he brings his blessings into your life so you can build his kingdom. When we give not to gain value but simply out of the overflow of God's love for us, we are free to love others and walk in our purpose.

## It's Your Choice—How Will You Use Your Gifts?

The Dream Builder has given you the gift of life. He has provided you with talents and abilities to fulfill a purpose. What you do with your life is your gift back to God.

God's gifts and call are irrevocable (Romans 11:29). Those treasures inside you are yours for life. Your gifts are yours, but what you do with them is your choice.

In the beginning of his life, Solomon used his God-given wisdom to govern and guide the people. He gave them a beautiful temple to worship the Lord. However, somewhere along the path he walked, there was a shift. Instead of using his assets for God's kingdom, Solomon began to use his gifts in a passionate pursuit of self. Near the end of his journey, Solomon realized his life had been filled with accomplishments, but so many of them were meaningless. As he looked back over his life and its worldly greatness, he noted it was "meaningless," "a chasing after the wind" (Ecclesiastes 2:26).

God gives gifts, talents, and treasures to all his children. The question is, what are you using them for? How will you use them to leverage and influence his kingdom?

## What Will You Say About Your Life?

Solomon had everything and yet nothing. At the end of his life, he determined his pursuit of self had been meaningless. Joseph lost everything and yet his life ended by bringing meaning to this world. Joseph told his brothers, "You intended to harm me, but God intended it for good to accomplish what is now being done, the saving of many lives" (Genesis 50:20).

What do you want to say about your life as you approach the end? Draw your value from the Dream Builder, and from that place of abundance share your gifts with others for his glory. This is freedom. Your heart for his glory.

*"My daughter, you have the treasure of Christ inside you. I have given you gifts, and I am waiting until your hands are willing to use your treasures for my glory alone. You have no idea what is inside you, and I am waiting to unleash this in your life when you are ready to serve me—not to prove your worth but to love others.*

*Do not listen to hate. My voice is wiser, better. I chose you. I built you. I will guard you. Those who accuse you have nothing to do with your dream.*

*You already have significance and matter greatly. Look to me to get your value. Look to me to find your dream. I am the only source from which they flow. When you look to others to find your worth, you will always come up empty.*

*I have said it . . . but my sweet child, you must believe it again and again and again. You are my treasure, uniquely designed for a purpose."*

*She paused and faith rose up inside her. With a mustard seed of faith, she declared, "I am God's treasure, designed for a unique purpose."*

*She changed her beliefs, and the Dream Builder helped her take her eyes off herself.*

*She embraced her value from the Dream Builder, so she began to focus on other people and their need to know the truth. She told others he placed in her path, "You are God's treasure, uniquely designed for a purpose."*

*And for the rest of her life, she used her treasure to share God's love with others. She even helped those who hurt her.*

*Her life brought meaning to others . . . and the Dream Builder smiled.*

# VIDEO SESSION NOTES

# Chapter 4
# HER HEART
# FOR HIS GLORY

# DAY 1

Nourish Scripture: Genesis 39–41

### 1 PRAY.

Begin your time with God in prayer.

### 2 MEDITATE ON GOD'S WORD.

Using your Anchor of Truth Card* from last week's Nourish Notes, renew your mind on that truth. Quiet and focus your thoughts. Pray the truth. Say the truth. Meditate on God's truth.

### 3 TAKE THE *REVEAL* STEP OF THE NOURISH BIBLE STUDY METHOD.

Connect with Jesus by studying the Weekly Nourish Scripture and allowing the Holy Spirit to reveal truth in those verses. Prayerfully read over and reflect on the passage. Mark any phrases, verses, or words that catch your attention. Journal and learn as the Lord leads you.

---

*Anchor of Truth Cards are available at www.TreasuredMinistries.com/shop

# DAY 2

Nourish Scripture: Genesis 39–41

**① PRAY.**

Begin your time with God in prayer.

**② MEDITATE ON GOD'S WORD.**

Using your Anchor of Truth Card* from last week's Nourish Notes, renew your mind on that truth. Quiet and focus your thoughts. Pray the truth. Say the truth. Meditate on God's truth.

**③ TAKE THE *RESPOND* STEP OF THE NOURISH BIBLE STUDY METHOD.**

Respond to activate truth in your life. The acronym **IMPACT** provides questions to help you apply the truth from your weekly Nourish Scripture. **Sometimes you may not have answers for all six questions.**

**I**MAGE OF GOD TO TRUST? An attribute of God, Jesus, or the Holy Spirit to trust.

**M**ESSAGE TO SHARE? A word of encouragement, truth, or prayer to share.

**P**ROMISE TO TREASURE? A promise in the Bible to believe.

**A**CTION TO TAKE? A specific step God is calling you to take.

**C**ORE IDENTITY IN CHRIST TO AFFIRM? A truth about how God sees you to affirm.

**T**RANSGRESSION TO CONFESS? A sin to acknowledge for help, healing, and restoration through Christ.

*Anchor of Truth Cards are available at www.TreasuredMinistries.com/shop

# DAY 3

Nourish Scripture: Genesis 39–41

**1 PRAY.**

Begin your time with God in prayer.

**2 MEDITATE ON GOD'S WORD.**

Using your Anchor of Truth Card* from last week's Nourish Notes, renew your mind on that truth. Quiet and focus your thoughts. Pray the truth. Say the truth. Meditate on God's truth.

**3 TAKE THE *RENEW* STEP OF THE NOURISH BIBLE STUDY METHOD.**

Like an anchor that secures its vessel, biblical meditation secures truth to transform your life. Take five minutes to *renew* your mind by focusing on one word, verse, or truth that the Holy Spirit revealed through the Bible during your week of study. Record your truth below and on your Anchor of Truth card.* Quiet your thoughts. Focus on the truth. Read the truth. Pray the truth.

My Anchor of Truth

**4 UTILIZE YOUR *ANCHOR OF TRUTH* CARD AS A BOOKMARK TO CULTIVATE A DAILY PRACTICE OF BIBLICAL MEDITATION.**

Place your Anchor of Truth Card* in your Bible study workbook to bookmark tomorrow's day of study. Let your Anchor of Truth bookmark remind you to pause and renew your mind on God's Word. Repeat this process daily, continuing to reflect on your Anchor of Truth to start your quiet time until the next week, when God reveals another truth to you.

*Anchor of Truth Cards are available at www.TreasuredMinistries.com/shop

# DAY 4

If God is for us, who can be against us?
—*Romans 8:31*

Young Joseph caught the eye of Potiphar's wife, and she sought after the handsome young servant. Instead of using her influence for good purposes, she wielded her power to satisfy her own desires. How long did Joseph serve in Potiphar's house before she decided to seduce him? Was there intimidation in the inflection of her voice as she boldly invited Joseph to come to her bed? Day after day, with persistence and manipulation, she did her best to wear down Joseph and gain control over him. But Joseph stood strong in the Lord. Finally, in an act of desperation, she grabbed Joseph's arm, presumably to embrace him. But he squirmed out of his cloak and fled the house, leaving her embarrassed and wrathful.

With the cloak as her evidence, she crafted a lie to cover her shame. He had fully rejected her, and now he would pay. This time, instead of being hurled into a pit, he was thrown into a prison. Although Potiphar's wife was more powerful than Joseph, she was no match for the Dream Builder. God was with Joseph, and God is with you.

*If God is for us, who can be against us?*

## Whom Shall I Fear?

Potiphar's wife may have been a young beauty, a physical peer to Joseph. If that was the case, I am sure Joseph's body was crying out to give in, yet he refused. Or perhaps she was middle-aged or unattractive. Even so, from the world's point of view, his position and security were in her hands, but still Joseph refused. This inspires me. What was the source of his courage? In one line of Scripture, we receive a life-changing revelation.

> "How then could I do such a wicked thing and sin against God?" And though she spoke to Joseph day after day, he refused to go to bed with her or even be with her. (Genesis 39:9–10)

While Potiphar's wife was powerful, God's influence in Joseph's life was exponentially greater. Even though Joseph was afraid, he chose to do the right thing. *He was more afraid to sin by refusing God than he was to refuse Potiphar's wife.* The world would have seen Potiphar and his wife as the source of Joseph's success, but Joseph knew his real source. God was the source of his courage, his strength, and his convictions. He knew Potiphar's wife was small compared with the God of Abraham. Joseph feared the Lord more than he feared people.

For Joseph, living for God's glory also meant telling the truth even when it was hard. He had the courage to share interpretations of dreams, no matter the cost—even when that meant sharing bad news with Pharaoh himself. He did not play politics or favor people because of their position; he served the prisoners just as faithfully as the palace dwellers. He trusted God because he knew God is bigger than anyone.

## Fear of the Lord Brings Courage to Carry Out Your Calling

Who are you living for? You were created to live for God's glory—not for pleasing people. Living in fear of people will paralyze your life purpose. There will always be those who are like Potiphar's wife: manipulators and intimidators standing in the pathway of your dream. These people can be very powerful against you, but not against your Dream Builder, who is always with you.

You will never have a life free of all manipulators, controllers, and intimidators ... but you *can* change your perception of these people. You have the power within you to say no to people so you can say yes to God. Satan works through people, and he would love to send you just the right people to tempt you to destroy your destiny (Ephesians 6:11–12). If you fear people, you are easy prey, so don't allow people to have power over you; flip your perspective—they are here for you to love!

Today is the day to make a decision about who will build your dream: God or people? God has given us a way to release our fear of people: changing our perspective. There is more than one way to see God, and more than one way to see even the most intimidating person.

How does Isaiah 51:12–16 challenge you to change your perception of fearing people versus fearing God?

_____

_____

_____

Proverbs 1:7 says, "The fear of the LORD is the beginning of knowledge." This knowledge includes a right perspective on life: God is the only one whose opinion matters. This knowledge brings courage where we were timid and freedom where we allowed ourselves to be in chains. Without the chains of pleasing others, you can follow God into the destiny he has designed for your life.

But God is love, so why should we fear him? We're not talking about fearing for your well-being as if God were unstable or threatening. He's not like the ocean or a tame lion that's safe one minute and will destroy you the next. To fear the Lord God is a Hebrew phrase that means to revere him—to hold him in the most important place in your life. It is being in awe of his greatness, majesty, and holiness. It causes you to live your life to serve him alone—a resolution to live for his glory.

## Choose Whom You Will Serve

When Joseph refused Potiphar's wife, it seemed at first that he lost everything: his reputation, his title, his freedom. He even lost the clothes on his back. It seemed as though Potiphar's wife had ruined him. Let this be a reminder that obedience and living for God's glory does not mean the absence of adversity. Far from it! The biblical writers impress upon us multiple times that following God is harder, not easier, than following the world. Matthew 7:13–23 has a clear message regarding this from Jesus himself. Jesus says following him is hard, and few can even find the road. He tells us there are many who will lead us astray, and many who think they've followed the Lord only to find they haven't! Not to mention earlier in 5:11 when he tells us we will be insulted, persecuted, and lied about because of living for him. So is there any benefit to living for God? YES! It's so much more fulfilling to live a life of purpose—a dream created just for you.

So don't be afraid to let go. The most important thing in life is to stay inside God's will. If that means losing what you have, then remember he has something better! As long as you have God, you have everything you need.

Remember: your Dream Builder is a rebuilder. No matter the cost, don't be afraid to say "No!" to people so you can say "Yes!" to God. Many women stay in abusive relationships because they are afraid of losing provision or perceived protection. Many women become entangled in possessive friendships and are afraid to cut ties with a woman who seems powerful (2 Timothy 3:6–7). When you first say no, you may experience hardship, but God always has the final say.

God will rescue, restore, redeem. Joseph was not a victim. He humbled himself under God's mighty hand, and in due time God lifted him up for his purpose (1 Peter 5:6–7). As Joseph sat in prison, it seemed that Potiphar's wife was still in control. But the Dream Builder, in his own time and in his own way, rescued Joseph from prison. In one moment, the Lord promoted Joseph to second in command in Egypt. In one moment God can redeem what was lost in a lifetime. You can always trust God. Everything Joseph touched flourished. God gave him favor and success. Joseph knew God was the source of his blessing, and so he was free to serve God alone.

If God has asked you to stand up to someone or break off a relationship, it is important to keep trusting him even when it looks as though things are falling apart. Walk by faith and not by sight—your Dream Builder is a rebuilder.

The names of Joseph's children captured the goodness of God. God erased all the trouble people had caused Joseph in his life. His first son's name, *Manasseh*, means "causing to forget." Because God made him fruitful in the land of his suffering, Joseph named his second son Ephraim. *Ephraim* means "double land" or "twice fruitful." God was faithful not only to restore Joseph but also to lift him up to new levels of influence where he could do God's work on a grand scale.[1] This reminds me of God's faithfulness to the Israelites after they returned from captivity in Babylon.

Instead of your shame you will receive a double portion, and instead of disgrace you will rejoice in your inheritance. And so you will inherit a double portion in your land, and everlasting joy will be yours. (Isaiah 61:7)

God restored Joseph more than double for his trouble. Joseph was not a victim, and neither are you.

## Fear of People Leads to Manipulating Others

The desire to please people over the Lord manifests itself in many ways: Sinning to go along with the crowd. Not saying what we believe because we are afraid of what others may think. Following those who are popular. Seeking the approval of or acting differently around those with money or position because we think they have the power to bless us. Trying to get what we want through flattery, manipulation, or other measures. Living with a thought life dominated by the fear of rejection, humiliation, or pain others may cause in our lives. Depending on others for security, significance, and strength. Needing the approval of others at all times because we are looking to people and not the Lord for our identity. Feeling distracted and at a standstill when others are not happy with us. Feeling "less than" around others who put us down. We can become so focused on wanting what people can give, we fail to see the many ways God is already giving us good things. Bitterness and unforgiveness prevail because we think people are the source of our blessing and therefore owe us.[2]

## Living for God's Glory Leads to Loving and Serving Others

When we live for God's glory, our lives are different: We look to others as people to love and serve—not to fear and please. Jesus showed us how to do this healthily. He always served, though not as a doormat. He turned to his Father for guidance (John 8:28–29). Then he determined his schedule and plans based on what he thought was best, not solely on the wants and needs of others. He used the word no without guilt because love does not mean always saying yes.

When we live for God's glory, we share the gospel with bold faith. Walking in forgiveness is easier because we look to the Lord as our source of blessing, not to people. We can pray for others to receive God's blessings. We are aware of and grateful for what God has given us. We are more focused on pleasing the Lord than pleasing people in our thoughts, words, and deeds. Our motives to serve are pure and unconditional. We desire to bring God glory and seek his will for our lives. We can accept responsibility for our mistakes and accept our identity and forgiveness from Christ. We look to God for our security, significance, and strength.[3]

How is your focus on other people keeping you from your spiritual inheritance? Are you blaming others for blocking your dreams? The problem is not with the people—it is with our perspective of people.

From Psalm 34 and this week's Scripture passage, answer the following questions.

In Psalm 34:7–16, what are the blessings of those who fear the Lord?

_____

_____

How did God encamp around Joseph?

_____

_____

How and when did God deliver Joseph?

_____

_____

Joseph had an important position in Potiphar's house. When he lost that position and was unjustly accused and imprisoned, how did God restore more than double for his trouble?

_____

_____

Joseph's obedience to God ushered him into prison at first. Living for God's glory does not mean the absence of adversity. How does Joseph's story encourage you to trust God? How could you use this story to encourage someone who is fearful of saying no to an abuser?

_____

_____

## Past Hurts Can Lead Us to Seek People Over God

While all of us struggle with fear of people to some extent, the degree to which that fear affects us usually stems from past hurts. If someone in your life, especially someone with authority, hurt you, he or she likely created a perception in your mind that people are more powerful than God. You may also have the impression that God is not loving. *If God loves me, why did he let this happen?* The greater your hurt and the deeper the wound, the greater your vulnerability will be to seek people over the Lord. If you seek to control them—or to please them—instead of resting under God's care, you are focusing on people. This sets up a vicious cycle as you place your hope in what people can give you and get hurt repeatedly. If you live your life this way, you will always feel like a victim because people are always imperfect.[4]

Joseph was sexually assaulted. He was able to escape but not without being punished by Potiphar's wife. Sometimes escape is not an option. Maybe you were forcefully trapped by a predator. Or maybe you were only a child and you didn't know you were being abused.

Perhaps you have not been sexually abused, but you have been mistreated verbally or physically. Perhaps you found yourself entangled by a person who wanted possession over your life, leading to emotional abuse. Your perception of people and God changed. You felt abandoned. Ashamed. Alone. Angry.

## Don't Let the Past Control Your Life

God cares about you.

Although the affliction may be over and perhaps that person is even out of your life, your attacker may still control your life. Like Joseph, you may find yourself in a prison. The bars are not physical but just as confining and unjust. They are the cold steel bars of shame, self-protection, anger, fear of rejection, unforgiveness, and pain.

Or maybe they're the bars of wrongly placed guilt. Are you accusing yourself for someone else's sin in your life? Joseph was not responsible for Potiphar's wife's actions, and you are not responsible for the actions of those who hurt you. God did not abandon you during that time. God is not ashamed of you. God loves you beyond measure and will redeem your hurts as you trust in him. Whatever the bars around you, the self-imposed prison is stealing your dream! It's time to arise and stand tall!

Dear daughter of the Dream Builder, Jesus has the keys! Take him by the hand in prayer and determine that you will not waste one more day inside that cell. He has a dream he wants to build through you.

If you are still being abused, please do not wait another day before you make a change. If you need help with knowing how to respond to any kind of abuse, you can call the National Domestic Violence Hotline at 1-800-799-SAFE. God's will for you is freedom and joy—and he will help you find both. Choose today to trust him.

## Choose to Be a Victor, Not a Victim

The Dream Builder longs to rescue you. Jesus came to bring justice to the injustices in your life. What God did in Joseph's life, he can do in yours. He longs to set you free—and he is more than able. He is waiting with open arms to comfort and heal you ... to set you free. Surrender your hurt to him. Let go of the shame. Don't allow the giants in your life to control you any longer. Turn to Jesus. You do not have the power to rescue yourself. Neither can other people. Jesus is the only answer. Don't be afraid to trust him. Choose to be a victim no more.

Yahweh. God. The Lord is his name. King of Kings. Lord of Lords. He is a strong tower. A fortress. He is mighty to save. The winds and waves obey his commands. "Holy, holy, holy is the Lord God Almighty, who was, and is, and is to come" (Revelation 4:8). He is Lord over all. "For from him and through him and for him are all things" (Romans 11:36).

Today is a new day. It's time to take back control by giving it to the only one worthy of worship. Jesus holds the keys that can unlock the doors of your prison. Trust God and surrender your heart to the One who is mighty to save. May you rest in his mighty hand as he recaptures your heart.

# DAY 5

Blessed is the one who trusts in the LORD, whose confidence is in him.
—*Jeremiah 17:7*

The purpose of every God-given dream is to bring glory to God. When God has our hearts completely and freely, his glory reigns and our freedom begins. Bringing yourself glory will never fulfill you. You were designed for something greater. Your heart was made for more—your heart for his glory. True success in God's eyes is taking hold of God's purpose for your life by allowing the Dream Builder to take hold of you. Fulfillment will find you when you seek God and live for him.

Sometimes you have to surrender your dream to find his dream for your life.

## Joseph's Rite of Passage Birthed a Life Lived for God's Glory

Like a baby bird shoved from its secure nest to learn how to fly, Joseph's journey continued as he was forced to spread his wings of faith in the God of his forefathers. Pushed out of his comfort zone and thrown into a different culture, he faced new challenges and foes but found that his God was bigger than his circumstances. From shepherd to slavery, sent to prison, and finally promoted to second in command in Egypt, Joseph was molded into the man God needed to carry out his dream. Glancing back over the thirteen years compacted into this week's three Bible chapters, I am moved to say in agreement with 1 Timothy 1:17, "To God be the glory."

The pit was Joseph's rite of passage that purified his heart and birthed a life lived for God's glory. After he was rescued, Joseph used his gifts to serve others at every turn. In our scripture this week Joseph was afflicted, yet he continued to live for God's glory whether he was in prison or palace. As Joseph humbled himself, God lifted him up so God could bless others through Joseph. Only when God is larger than our lives will we truly live. Joseph had many reasons to stop believing in the goodness of God and close his heart to him, yet he continued to trust the Dream Builder. His faith was truly remarkable!

Let's review two truths we learned in chapter 2.

1. When God reigns in the heart of a woman, his glory will illuminate the path of her purpose and she will be free to step into the spacious place of her God-given dream that has already been planned for her (Romans 12:2; Psalm 16:5–7; Jeremiah 29:11; Ephesians 2:10).

2. Worship makes God bigger, and our idols simply lose their luster. Worship promotes truth over lies in our minds and builds an altar to God in our hearts where we can sacrifice the things that hold us back from him.

It's not enough to leave your idols—you must live for God's glory.

Whether in the prison or the palace, Joseph lived for God's glory. This is the key to God building his dream through you. It's not enough to stop living for yourself or for people, possessions, or positions. You have to replace your previous passion, or it will slowly take its place on the throne again. Allow the discomfort you feel in dethroning your idol to fuel the fire of your passion for God and for living for him. Just think: God desires to display his splendor through you (Isaiah 61:3). When you give to others out of the fullness of what God has given to you, the Dream Builder will begin to rebuild his dream through you (Isaiah 58:8–10).

Oh holy, precious truth! You, brave heart, were created to bring him glory, and your heart will never rest until you do. Your God-given purpose is to live for his glory.

## Changing Our Perspective Will Bring Us to Our Knees Before God

Come on a journey with me as we peer into this week's passage and Psalm 34 to change our perspective of God. "Glorify the LORD with me; let us exalt his name together" (Psalm 34:3). God never changes. He is sovereign and all-powerful, seated on the throne of glory! However, when we perceive him as small, we dethrone him in our minds and hearts. Magnifying and glorifying God is life-changing because it corrects our skewed perspective of God and gives us courage to surrender our hearts to his mighty, all-embracing love.

Reflect on this week's Bible passages, Psalm 34 and Genesis 39–41, and answer the following questions.

From our story this week, list some ways Joseph was afflicted by other people or by his circumstances.

_____

_____

_____

_____

How did Joseph give glory to God at all times? (Psalm 34:1)

_____

_____

_____

How did Joseph reflect the Lord's radiance to others in Potiphar's house, in prison, and in the palace? (Psalm 34:5)

_____

_____

_____

_____

What evidence do you see that the Lord was Joseph's sole source of strength and success?

_____

_____

_____

_____

Where do you see Joseph's humility?

_____

_____

_____

_____

God sees the afflicted and hears their cries for rescue. God loves his children beyond measure. Where do you see that God is close to the brokenhearted and afflicted and cares when evil is done to them?

_____

_____

_____

_____

What passage in Psalm 34 reveals that God is our sole source of blessing beyond measure and is the only one worthy of our worship?

_____

_____

_____

_____

From Psalm 34:19, how much trouble did God say the righteous would have? How does trouble shake your faith? How do these verses encourage you to take refuge in him and walk by faith when you cannot see God's hand in your life?

_____

_____

_____

_____

How have you tasted and seen the Lord's goodness in your life recently? How has God taken care of you in times of trouble or "famine"?

_____

_____

_____

_____

God was everything to Joseph. On every platform large or small, Joseph gave glory to God and was a channel of God's blessing to others. His view of God affected his actions, aligning him for God's purpose in his life. Joseph was not a victim of his afflictions—his heart was in the hands of one who loved and blessed him beyond measure.

## Joseph Recognized God's Power and His Own Limitations

The Lord was with Joseph and gave him success in everything he did (Genesis 39:3). God also granted Joseph favor in Potiphar's household, in the prison, and finally in Pharaoh's palace. It was the Lord who gave him blessing, favor, and success.

Joseph realized his own limitations, and so he recognized the power of God working through him as he experienced this success. Last week we saw that God gifted Joseph with amazing wisdom and the ability to interpret dreams. But Joseph never forgot his dependence on God—even in the use of his gifts.

When Pharaoh came to him to interpret his dreams, Joseph used his platform to declare God's goodness to the ruler of Egypt: "I cannot do it ... but God will give Pharaoh the answer he desires" (Genesis 41:16). When Pharaoh's cupbearer and baker came to him for an interpretation of their dreams, Joseph responded by saying, "Do not interpretations belong to God?" (Genesis 40:8). Because of Joseph's humility, others saw God's Spirit working through him mightily. Pharaoh declared, "Can we find anyone like this man, one in whom is the Spirit of God?" (Genesis 41:38).

## Are You Missing Out on "Beyond Measure"?

God was with Joseph, and he is with you. Having the Holy Spirit inside you is not the same as allowing the Holy Spirit to have all of you. Why would you place your heart in the hands of people, possessions, positions, or even yourself? Place your heart in the hands of the living God, who provides for you beyond measure.

> Now to him who is able to do *immeasurably more* than all we ask or imagine, according to his power that is at work within us, to him be glory in the church and in Christ Jesus throughout all generations, for ever and ever! (Ephesians 3:20–21, *emphasis mine*)

The God you serve is an "immeasurably more" God. Joseph saw fruitfulness flow from his hands that was "beyond measure" and he used his influence to give to others (Genesis 41:49). God taught Joseph to depend solely on him. When he was placed in charge of the whole land of Egypt, he was ready (Genesis 41:41). He used his position and provision to serve and save all of Egypt and many in the surrounding regions, including his own family! He glorified God by using his wisdom, wealth, and influence to save the lives of many.

God wants to bless us beyond measure in ways that are sometimes different from our ideas (Isaiah 55:8). Following God may feel risky, but when we cling to whatever else we believe will bring us happiness while giving God only half our hearts, we don't guarantee a life of control and calm. We only guarantee that we'll miss out on far more than we ever imagined. Isn't giving God your whole heart worth it?

*Kardia*, the Greek word we translate as "heart," means "the centre and seat of spiritual life, the soul or mind, as it is the fountain and seat of the thoughts, passions, desires, appetites, affections, purposes, endeavors."[5] Yielding my heart means choosing "to let God meet my needs in the ways he sees best, not in the ways in which I want to see things done. I decide to trust and look to Him as the source of my contentment, joy, and security, instead of looking to circumstances and to other people."[6]

## The Scriptures Promise Problems—and Deliverance

Life will never be fair but it can be better than good when you live for his glory. In his book *Better Than Good*, Zig Ziglar tells the story of Vice Admiral James Stockton. Stockton was a POW in the Vietnam War. Ziglar writes,

> He did not consider his captivity to be a failure on his part. He viewed it as an opportunity to continue doing what he had done throughout his career—providing leadership wherever he was assigned.[7]

Where has God assigned you? Adversity is a part of life. Yes, adversity can be painful, but it never signifies the absence of his love! If you are waiting for God to make life fair so you can give him your heart, you will be waiting the rest of your life. Remember, the Scriptures promise the righteous will have many problems, but God will deliver them (Psalm 34:19). He sees your afflictions and hears your cries for rescue. He will rebuild, restore, and redeem your shame. He has good things for you. You can trust him with your heart and with your greatest desires.

The enemy whispered lies in Eve's ear: *Trust in your own heart. Be your own god. God is holding back on you. Take the glory!* Today he comes with the same lies. Satan will tell you not to yield control of your life to God. Trusting in self naturally yields a focus on you. Then your emotions and feelings will determine your "needs." These needs quickly become demands that lead to decreasing God's role in your life and increasing your own. And as you take control, you miss out on "beyond measure" . . . a life lived for the glory of God.

## Trust the Only One Who Can Bless You Beyond Measure

Searching for happiness inside yourself, other people, or your circumstances drains your heart and is an endless, meaningless pursuit of the things of this world. The secret is to surrender your heart, seek God, and trust your loving Father to give you what you need.

Your heart is an unbelievable treasure to God, but you will never be free until he has all your heart. When I think about my heart—my most valuable possession—do I want to cling to it and enjoy measured success at best? Or do I want to trust the one who can bless me beyond measure so I can be a blessing to others?

Your heart for his glory. Surrender and live God's dream for your life.

# DAY 6

Glory in his holy name; let the hearts of those who seek the LORD rejoice.
—*Psalm 105:3*

Before we begin, I would like to share my heart with you about this chapter. Each chapter is a piece of my journey with the Lord. Just like you, I am on a journey through his Word, led by the Holy Spirit, cutting new pathways through the dark forest of confusion and allowing the truth to light my steps as I find my way into the great expanse of his freedom (Psalm 119:45). This chapter, however, represents a turning point for me like no other. I have never felt so compelled, yet inadequate, to write on the subject the Lord laid before me. I have never cried out louder to God. I have never sought friends more diligently to pray for me. I have never seen the depths of my heart and my sin so deeply . . . I have never experienced such joy. Writing this chapter would begin a "rite of passage" in my own walk with the Lord to bring my heart closer to his. With this study, a season began that would change my life.

I was still holding part of my heart back from God. I thought I knew what would make me happy—and what if God did not come through? This strategy for living offered no freedom. It only tied my soul to my limited thinking, which restricted my ability to bless others. Yet I continued. I continued clinging to my heart, my dreams, even more tightly.

What I was missing was greater than what I had. I had my desires, my dreams, and my own agenda, but I was missing living for God's glory. I was feasting on a fare that could never fill me. God desired that I delight in the richest of fare and satisfy my thirst with his nourishing milk and extravagant wine (Isaiah 55:1–2).

Weary from the endless pursuit of striving to take care of myself, I found myself resting in God's arms again. I was broken with nothing to give him but my heart. But that was all he wanted. When I surrendered that bit of my heart that thought I knew best, I found freedom and I was filled to overflowing. I cannot explain this divine exchange, except that he truly provides the richest of fare to nourish our souls.

Your heart for his glory. This is the purpose for God's dream for your life. Fear of people places shackles on souls and can lead to unhealthy dependence on relationships. Living for our glory keeps us bound. But living for God's glory with our hearts surrendered to him brings freedom. Every bit of your heart you surrender to God becomes ground he can use to rebuild his dream in your life. The more you surrender, the bigger and better he can build.

The answer is not simply to change your behavior. To dethrone your idol of people and put God on the throne of your heart, you will need to change your beliefs about God, others, and yourself. Only then will you be able to see God's perfect will for your life (Romans 12:1–2).

## Only a Surrendered Heart Brings Abundant Life

We all worship something—we were built to worship. Whatever we give our heart to becomes our god. It's what we serve. It's what we worship. It's ultimately what controls us. We can't have two gods, only one. When you perceive others or yourself and your desires as more important than God, you've made your choice. Then you will be separated from the most important part of your provision—the Lord Almighty himself! Choosing where to give your heart is a life-changing decision.

## Compare Two Paths—and Choose One

Today is a day for personal reflection and a chance to declare victory by surrendering your heart to God and choosing to worship him. The next two pages detail two pathways for your heart. Take some time to ponder over each pathway and honestly consider your life as it is, not as you'd like it to be. Allow God to take you on a deep journey into the depths of your heart by praying before you begin.

Following the charts are questions to consider and journal your thoughts. Don't feel confined to the questions. Allow them to inspire your thoughts as you write the words God is whispering to your heart. I encourage you to close out your time with the prayer of surrender at the end. Live for his glory and enter the abundant life God designed you to have!

# MY HEART FOR HIS GLORY

**IMPERFECT PEOPLE, CIRCUMSTANCES, AND CHOICES HURT MY HEART**
*Psalm 73:26; Mark 4:18–20; Romans 3:9–1*

**MY WOUNDED HEART REAFFIRMS BELIEFS BASED ON GOD'S WORD. I STAND ON THE TRUTH.**
*Prov. 30:5; John 1:17; 8:32; Gal. 5:1; Eph. 6:14; Heb. 11:1; John 4:50*

**I BELIEVE GOD**
- Sees my afflictions. He hears my cries for help. He loves me always. I will praise him. *Gen. 29:31–35; Psalm 34:1–5, 15–18; Isaiah 54:10; John 16:33*
- Is my sole source for beyond measure blessings; and worthy of my worship. *Psalm 34:8–10, 37:4–5; Eph. 3:20*
- Is my vindicator; as I trust in him, he will redeem, restore, rescue, and rebuild. *Psalm 34:4–7, 19–22; Isaiah 41:8–14, 54:17, 61:7; Mark 10:29–31; 2 Thess. 1:6*

**I BELIEVE PEOPLE**
- Are imperfect and have measured power. *Jer. 17:5–9; John 10:11–13; Rom. 8:31–32*
- Are here for me to love as Christ loved me. *Luke 6:35–38; Eph. 5:1–8; Phil. 2:1–11*
- Are forgivable; I release people and receive from God. *Matt. 18:21–22*
- Are not meant to be worshiped so I can walk away from unhealthy relationships. *1 Cor 15:33; Romans 1:25*

**I BELIEVE I**
- Can trust my loving Father to give me what I need when I need it. *Matt 6:33, 2 Cor. 5:15*
- Should follow God. He has the best plan for my life. *Prov. 3:4–6; Isaiah 58:11–12; Jer. 29:11; Mark 8:31–37*
- Am more than a conqueror because I am trusting the Lord completely. *Num. 14:9; Rom. 8:35–39*
- Can rest from fear through my faith in Christ. *Phil. 4:13; Psalm 27:1; Rom. 8: 14–17*
- Am who God says I am. In Christ, I am forgiven, loved, accepted, worthy, God's chosen treasure, his child, ambassador, completely covered from shame. I have purpose! *Psalm 23; 2 Cor. 13:4; Gal. 4:4–6; Eph. 2:4–5 & 10; 2 Tim. 2:7; Isaiah 43:1*
- Should keep my focus on Christ and bringing him glory. I am grateful for the glimpses of glory he brings to me. *Dan. 7:9–10, 13–14; Heb. 12:1–2*

**DESIRE TO SURRENDER AND TRUST GOD WITH MY HEART. GOD INCREASES. I LOSE MY LIFE TO FIND IT AND LOVE PEOPLE. I CAN CHOOSE TO OBEY THE HOLY SPIRIT, RESTING IN THE OVERFLOW OF HIS LOVE, STRENGTH, AND SUPPLY. I AM FREE.** *Matt. 10:39, 11:28–29; John 15:4, 12; Gal. 3:3, 5:1, 16–26*

**I CHOOSE TO REST UNDER GOD'S CARE**
God cares for my needs perfectly so I don't fear surrendering my life's dreams and desires to him. I seek him and trust him to give me what I need, when I need it. He wants to love and give to me beyond measure. He provides, promotes, and protects me perfectly. I don't have to control others to get what I want. I am free to forgive others because they owe me nothing. I freely give to others, trusting God to supply my needs. *Psalm 23*

**I CHOOSE TO REST UNDER GOD'S COVER**
God has covered all my sin and shame through Christ. I am accepted and loved no matter what. It's OK to make a mistake. I can accept responsibility for my sins by confessing them to God and getting the help I need. I can live with the disapproval of others because I have his approval always. His conviction is loving and for my good. *Heb. 10:4–11; 1 John 1:5–10*

**I CHOOSE TO REST UNDER GOD'S CONTROL**
The Good Shepherd leads me perfectly into his amazing plan for my life. I am led by the Spirit, not by guilt, manipulation, or my feelings. I surrender fearlessly knowing if God wants me to let go of anything, including my desires, he has the best plan. I make good choices that lead to abundant living. I am free to say no to people so I can say yes to God. I can speak the Truth in love to others because it's the Truth that sets me free. *Luke 6:37–38; John 10:1–10*

*I am saved and surrendered to a God who has amazing love for me. I live for God's glory and trust him for all things. Filled with God's perfect love and his strength, I rely on and spend time with him. I am focused on Christ and my life becomes an overflow of his overflow of his love to others. My heart is truly free. It's not about me, and my life is blessed beyond measure.*

*Kardia, the Greek word for heart, means: "the seat of spiritual life, the soul or mind, as it is the fountain and seat of the thoughts, passions, desires, appetites, affections, purposes, endeavors."*
*Luke 8:15*

# MY HEART AFRAID TO SURRENDER ALL

## IMPERFECT PEOPLE, CIRCUMSTANCES, AND CHOICES HURT MY HEART
*Psalm 73:26; Mark 4:18–20; Romans 3:9–1*

## MY WOUNDED HEART ESTABLISHES FALSE BELIEFS BASED ON HURTS. I LEAN ON LIES.
*John 8:44–47*

| I FALSELY BELIEVE GOD | • Is not loving because I have experienced trials.<br>• Abandoned me and is not protecting me because I was hurt.<br>• Is ashamed of me because of what has happened. He is angry and distant because of what I have done.<br>• Doesn't provide for me or have my best interest at heart. He does not really have a dream for me. |
|---|---|
| I FALSELY BELIEVE PEOPLE | • Have more power than God and are worthy of my fear.<br>• Are more loving than God.<br>• Are worthy of my worship. I give them undue authority over my life and become entangled in unhealthy relationships.<br>• Should be perfect, and I cannot forgive them when they break my trust.<br>• Are here to meet my needs and "owe me." |
| I FALSELY BELIEVE I | • Don't matter much to God. My life is not valuable, and I treat myself accordingly.<br>• Cannot receive God's blessings. I reject love from others.<br>• Need to stay in control to get what I want because I am fearful God may not come through.<br>• Should focus on my unmet demands and people who have disappointed me; therefore, I fail to see God's blessings in my life.<br>• Am a victim of imperfect people and circumstances.<br>• Should draw my value from what others say about me, worldly standards, my performance, my background, or my ability. |

## BELIEFS ROOTED IN LIES CREATE FEAR, WHICH DRIVES DESIRES INTO DEMANDS. GOD DECREASES, AND I LIVE FOR MYSELF. MY HEART IS CAPTIVE TO PEOPLE AND THINGS. I AM WEARY. THE CYCLE CONTINUES AND I MISS THE BLESSING OF SURRENDERING MY HEART.
*Matt. 11:28–29; Gal. 3:3, 5:16–21*

| I CHOOSE TO RELY ON OTHERS AND MYSELF **FOR CARE.** | I believe that God may not come through for me so I need to take matters in my own hands. I believe the strength and provision people can provide is more powerful than God. I manipulate, flatter, and please others. I play favorites with people who have money, position, or perceived power. I am bitter, depressed, and angry because I trust in an imperfect measured source. I need to vindicate and repay my hurt. People owe me for the hurts in my life. I must take what I need. I see people for what I can get. I need to control others. I don't listen to God to take time to nourish myself—body, soul, and spirit—so I am worn and have nothing to give others. I reject God's blessings in my life. |
|---|---|
| I CHOOSE TO RELY ON OTHERS AND MYSELF **FOR COVER.** | I need others to tell me I am acceptable and so I need to please others. It's hard to hear criticism. I perform to get the daily affirmation I need. I need to cover my shame so I must be perfect. If I make a mistake, I blame others instead of taking responsibility. The cross was not enough so I must "punish" myself for my mistakes by cutting myself, negative self-talk, not taking care of myself, closing the door to God's blessings in my life, or other destructive measures. I also take on the shame of others, and especially those who hurt me. I am restless and distracted or "paralyzed" when those close to me are disappointed in me. |
| I CHOOSE TO RELY ON MYSELF AND OTHERS **FOR CONTROL.** | I fear disappointing people, so they control my life. Instead of receiving abundant life, I follow other voices that cannot love me like God can. I have a hard time making decisions, or allow others to make them for me. I fear stating my own opinion. I have trouble setting boundaries. I don't believe it's OK to say no. I think I know what's best so my agenda and my expectations drive my steps and decisions. I miss out on God's best for my life. My soul is tied to bad relationships. I have a hard time trusting the Holy Spirit's still small voice in my life and become quickly double-minded when I listen to other people, look to my circumstances, or try to figure everything out. |

*I am saved but not surrendered. I live for myself because I am afraid to trust God. I rely on my measured strength and become weary. I look to people and get hurt and let down. I am focused on my agenda, rights, and demands; I fear man. My heart is not free. I am unable to truly give to others. My life is about me and I am miserable.*

*Kardia, the Greek word for heart, means: "the seat of spiritual life, the soul or mind, as it is the fountain and seat of the thoughts, passions, desires, appetites, affections, purposes, endeavors"*
*Luke 8:15*

*Some thoughts are taken from Edward T. Welch, When People Are Big and God is Small: Overcoming Peer Pressure and the Fear of Man (Phillipsburg, N.J.: Presbyterian and Reformed Publishing Company, 1997)*

Compare the two paths and consider your life. What thoughts do you have? It's unlikely for a person to align with ALL the bullet points in each section. Where do you see your story?

_____

_____

_____

_____

What do these paths reveal about the state of your heart? Where do you feel you are currently walking?

_____

_____

_____

If you are surrendered, wonderful! Where can you surrender more? We are all growing and learning. If you are struggling to surrender, it's wonderful you are here, engaging with God. What is your greatest fear in surrendering?

_____

_____

_____

_____

What evidence can you find from your life, Joseph's life, and Psalm 34 about these truths:

God cares for us completely.

_____

_____

God covers our shame.

_____

_____

When God is in control of our lives and we take refuge in him, we will lack no good thing.

_____

_____

## Lay Down Your Life—Moment by Moment

If you choose, close today in a prayer of surrender. You cannot imagine the weight that is lifted off your heart when you choose to surrender to him! Every step you take in laying down your life is a spiritual act of worship to the One who laid his life down for yours.

*My Dream Builder,*

*I confess to you that I thought your care, cover, and your perfect capability to bring people into abundant living was for someone else. When I got hurt, I decided you didn't really love me as much as I could love myself. I took matters into my own hands, and I tried to do what only you can do for me.*

*I am tired of carrying my shame, and I surrender it to you. I believe you forgave me and see me as clean. I am worn-out from trying to care for myself. Only you can protect me and provide for me. I look to you, Good Shepherd, and choose today to come under your control and care as you lead and guide me. I release the hurts in my heart to you.*

*Show me any area I am not placing in the refuge of your loving staff that guides me and your rod that guards me. I have lived for myself, and I am not fulfilled. I confess that I have turned to people to get my needs met. They have become little idols that can never replace you. The world lied to me. The enemy has lied also, and I believed him. I chose to pursue my own definition of happiness instead of your glory.*

*You are my beyond-measure God, and the only life worth living is when you take me beyond myself. It's hard to turn from my idol of people because people are in my life all the time. So I'll just surrender and tell you that apart from you, I can do nothing—but with you, all things. I choose today to turn my eyes to you, Jesus, and trust you with whatever you're calling me to lay down, knowing you always have my best interest in mind. I give you the keys to my heart, for you have set my heart free.*

*Amen*

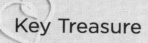

## Key Treasure

Every step you take in laying down your life is a spiritual act of worship to the One who laid his life down for yours.

# VIDEO SESSION NOTES

Session 4
## HER HEART FOR HIS GLORY
*Genesis 39–41*

Videos located online at www.nourishbiblestudyseries.com

# Chapter 5
# RECONCILIATION

# DAY 1

### Nourish Scripture: Genesis 42–45

## 1 PRAY.

Begin your time with God in prayer.

## 2 MEDITATE ON GOD'S WORD.

Using your Anchor of Truth Card* from last week's Nourish Notes, renew your mind on that truth. Quiet and focus your thoughts. Pray the truth. Say the truth. Meditate on God's truth.

## 3 TAKE THE *REVEAL* STEP OF THE NOURISH BIBLE STUDY METHOD.

Connect with Jesus by studying the Weekly Nourish Scripture and allowing the Holy Spirit to reveal truth in those verses. Prayerfully read over and reflect on the passage. Mark any phrases, verses, or words that catch your attention. Journal and learn as the Lord leads you.

*Anchor of Truth Cards are available at www.TreasuredMinistries.com/shop

# DAY 2

### Nourish Scripture: Genesis 42–45

**1 PRAY.**
Begin your time with God in prayer.

**2 MEDITATE ON GOD'S WORD.**
Using your Anchor of Truth Card* from last week's Nourish Notes, renew your mind on that truth. Quiet and focus your thoughts. Pray the truth. Say the truth. Meditate on God's truth.

**3 TAKE THE *RESPOND* STEP OF THE NOURISH BIBLE STUDY METHOD.**
Respond to activate truth in your life. The acronym **IMPACT** provides questions to help you apply the truth from your weekly Nourish Scripture. **Sometimes you may not have answers for all six questions.**

**I**MAGE OF GOD TO TRUST? An attribute of God, Jesus, or the Holy Spirit to trust.

**M**ESSAGE TO SHARE? A word of encouragement, truth, or prayer to share.

**P**ROMISE TO TREASURE? A promise in the Bible to believe.

**A**CTION TO TAKE? A specific step God is calling you to take.

**C**ORE IDENTITY IN CHRIST TO AFFIRM? A truth about how God sees you to affirm.

**T**RANSGRESSION TO CONFESS? A sin to acknowledge for help, healing, and restoration through Christ.

*Anchor of Truth Cards are available at www.TreasuredMinistries.com/shop

# DAY 3

Nourish Scripture: Genesis 42–45

**1 PRAY.**

Begin your time with God in prayer.

**2 MEDITATE ON GOD'S WORD.**

Using your Anchor of Truth Card* from last week's Nourish Notes, renew your mind on that truth. Quiet and focus your thoughts. Pray the truth. Say the truth. Meditate on God's truth.

**3 TAKE THE _RENEW_ STEP OF THE NOURISH BIBLE STUDY METHOD.**

Like an anchor that secures its vessel, biblical meditation secures truth to transform your life. Take five minutes to _renew_ your mind by focusing on one word, verse, or truth that the Holy Spirit revealed through the Bible during your week of study. Record your truth below and on your Anchor of Truth card.* Quiet your thoughts. Focus on the truth. Read the truth. Pray the truth.

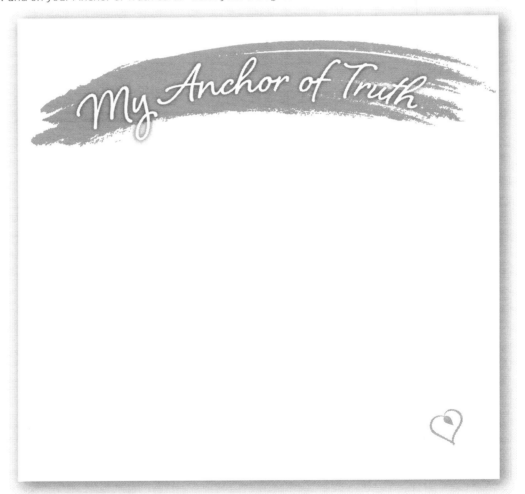

_My Anchor of Truth_

**4 UTILIZE YOUR _ANCHOR OF TRUTH_ CARD AS A BOOKMARK TO CULTIVATE A DAILY PRACTICE OF BIBLICAL MEDITATION.**

Place your Anchor of Truth Card* in your Bible study workbook to bookmark tomorrow's day of study. Let your Anchor of Truth bookmark remind you to pause and renew your mind on God's Word. Repeat this process daily, continuing to reflect on your Anchor of Truth to start your quiet time until the next week, when God reveals another truth to you.

*Anchor of Truth Cards are available at www.TreasuredMinistries.com/shop

# DAY 4

Be kind and compassionate to one another, forgiving each other,
just as in Christ God forgave you. —*Ephesians 4:32*

A famine would push Jacob and his family outside the perimeters of the Promised Land. As the food supplies diminished, Jacob knew he had to do something. While Jacob knew Canaan was the Promised Land, the family had to be saved. And so he sent his children down to Egypt to buy grain, unaware that this move was simply a stroke of the Dream Builder's design. God was getting ready to reunite Jacob's family. Joseph's family. Abraham's family. God's family of his chosen people.

So there they were. In Egypt, ten brothers finally bowed before Joseph and God's vision became reality. As Joseph glanced at his brothers for the first time in many years, did it trigger painful memories of the shackles on his feet? (Psalm 105:18). As his brothers lowered their heads before him, Joseph had a choice to make, a choice of such magnitude that it was history in the making. This choice was an opportunity. His hands held the power to save his family and bless them abundantly or pay back his brothers for their betrayal. Joseph had a choice. Forgiveness or revenge. Love or hate.

Joseph's choice to forgive his brothers' actions opened the door for complete restoration. He didn't save only his brothers—he saved the dream. Abraham's dream. God's dream. God's dream reached forward through the years—and throughout eternity. The Messiah would descend from Joseph's brother Judah.

## You Will Have Choices

As you walk out your God-given dream, you will have similar opportunities. At times, you too will be faced with a choice to forgive or seek revenge. Your choices will have far-reaching effects on you, on others, and on the fulfillment of your purpose.

In our fallen world of imperfect people and circumstances, our hearts are vulnerable to being hurt by others. Sometimes this hurt can come from the most unlikely places—a trusted friend, a family member, someone in a leadership position. The ones called to defend and protect us may let us down. The closer the person who offends us, the deeper the hurt.

When someone hurts us, like Joseph, we are faced with a choice. Forgiveness or revenge. Love or hate. When we forgive, we allow God's dream in our lives to continue. However, when we choose to hang on to offenses, we detour off God's path for us. Our bitterness toward others, instead of our love and devotion to God, begins to shape our thinking and our actions.

Read 2 Corinthians 2:10–11 and Ephesians 6:11–12. Whose schemes are you following when unforgiveness is influencing you? How do these scriptures motivate you to forgive others?

_____

_____

_____

How has unforgiveness reaped destruction in your own life and in the lives around you?

_____

_____

## Satan Works Through People to Destroy Us and Our Dream

Satan delights in using our grudges as tools to destroy our lives (2 Corinthians 2:10–11). He works through people to hurt us and put us in a self-imposed prison of unforgiveness (Ephesians 6:11–12; Matthew 18:21–35). Be aware, daughter of the Dream Builder. You are anointed for the amazing (John 14:12). Satan will try to use unforgiveness to prevent you from living God's dream for your life. When we nurse grudges, we play into Satan's hands, and our influence is wasted instead of being used for God's glory.

## The Opportunity of a Lifetime

Intertwined in our passage this week are priceless principles of forgiveness to explore. Joseph walked through a process of letting go of the past and choosing to love his brothers. Hate and unforgiveness can take over our lives, but God has given us a greater way.

Sometimes if we shift our focus on a matter, our perspective can change. Let's take a second look at forgiveness. Let's shift our focus and see offense as an opportunity to trust the Dream Builder.

## People Are Not Perfect, but God Is—Trust Him

Hurting people hurt others. Joseph's brothers were hurt and jealous because their father played favorites with Joseph. People are people. We all have faults. All fall short of the glory of God (Romans 3:10–12). No matter how wonderful people are, they are not perfect, and they have the potential to hurt us (John 2:24–25). God gives us free choice. Our choices can hurt others, and others can hurt us. However, if our faith is in God, we are free to love those God gives us to love—even those who have hurt us—as we surrender our hearts to him.

God is your defender (John 10:1–13; 1 Corinthians 13:6; Joshua 23:10; Exodus 14:14). He is your promise keeper (Joshua 23:14). He is your provider (Matthew 6:33; Philippians 4:19). He is the lover of your soul (Psalm 36:7). He gives you acceptance and abundance in his love and grace. This is where your trust needs to rest (John 2:24–25).

> A natural response to being hurt is to feel the offender owes us something. The debt could be anything. Think about a hurt you cannot seem to release. What does that person owe you? Money? Time? Your childhood? Your self-esteem? An apology? Your health? Your marriage? What has been stolen? Your dignity, self-respect, or reputation?

---
---
---

People who hurt us may never be able—or willing—to give us back what they took. However, we can forgive the debt, turn, and trust the Dream Builder to provide. Instead of looking to the offending person to restore what we lost, we need to look to Jesus. It is not our job to administer justice and make everything right and fair. People cannot restore what has been lost, but Jesus can.

Forgiveness is not saying what happened was acceptable or right. Forgiveness is saying, "I release you so I can receive from God." When we cling to unforgiveness, we are putting our faith in people coming through for us. But Jesus said, "Have faith in God" (Mark 11:22).

> Are you holding on to any unforgiveness? Where is your faith? Do you have a personal story of seeing God's release in your life because of forgiveness? Would you be willing to share with the group?

---
---
---

## Take Time Out

Joseph began his encounter with his brothers by speaking harshly to them. Dressed in clothing of his Egyptian culture, Joseph cleverly disguised himself with his sharp tongue and false accusations. I believe a part of Joseph was angry. He had every right to be angry. He had every right to deny them the help they needed. Why should he help them?

God in his grace kept the brothers from recognizing their brother as they bowed low to the ground. Joseph threw them into prison, giving himself some time with God instead of impulsively lashing out with regrettable actions. When we are angry, it is always better to walk away and not react. This allows us time to seek God and get his perspective on the situation and to renew our minds on the truth. We can ask the Lord how to deal with the situation instead of taking matters into our own hands.

Pulling away allows time to process your thoughts with God and pour your heart out to him. Don't use the time to justify your right to be angry or to rehearse what you will say to the offender. Use the time to ask the Holy Spirit to guide you and give you the strength and courage to forgive and walk in love.

## Surrender

God was not simply Joseph's Dream Builder, but his Lord. On the third day, he let his brothers out of prison and sent them away with provisions and their money because he "feared" God (Genesis 42:17–18).

Forgiveness is not merely a suggestion—it is a command, a step the Dream Builder wants you to take for your good. When you put the Dream Builder first in your life, you will walk in obedience to him, and his truth will set you free (John 8:32).

God is your Dream Builder—but only you can choose to make him Lord. Surrender and let the unforgiveness go!

## Pray for Those Who Hurt You

Joseph prepared a meal for his brothers (Genesis 43:16–17; Romans 12:20). He arranged for their feet to be washed (Genesis 43:24; John 13:12). He gave them undeserved provision and was above reproach when he returned their silver payment for the grain (Romans 12:14, 20).

What do you learn from these scriptures about loving your enemies?

Luke 6:32–36

_____

_____

_____

Romans 12:17–20

_____

_____

_____

Prayer is one of the greatest gifts you can give to others. As you pray, God can reveal to you why offenders did what they did and show you that they are broken like you. When you pray for those who hurt you, you are releasing them to God.

The Bible tells us to love our enemies and pray for them. Usually you won't have those warm fuzzy feelings to pray for your enemies as you do your friends! When someone has hurt you, you will probably not feel like praying for him or her. But don't wait until you feel like praying—make a choice to obey God. We receive our forgiveness and blessings from God by faith—not feelings—and we must offer forgiveness and love based on faith, not feelings.

The Holy Spirit will give you compassion as you pray, and he can show you how to pray for them as you allow him to pray through you.

## Forgiveness Builds Dreams

For Joseph and for us, complete forgiveness sometimes comes in layers. It is a process. Perhaps there are many layers wrapped so tightly around your heart you feel overwhelmed and do not know where to begin. Take the first step by going to Jesus in prayer.

You have a choice. Are you going to play into the enemy's schemes of hate—or trust the Dream Builder? The enemy does not have the keys to your dream. Trust the Dream Builder. Let all offense and bitterness go.

Forgiveness is an opportunity to open the doors to the Dream Builder's dream in our lives. An opportunity to restore our physical health. An opportunity to bring rest to our souls. An opportunity to unleash the Holy Spirit in our lives and love those around us.

Shift your thinking and change your focus. Your Dream Builder is waiting to help you. God was with Joseph and he is with you.

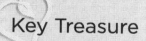

## Key Treasure

You have a choice. Are you going to play into the enemy's schemes of hate—or trust the Dream Builder? The enemy does not have the keys to your dream. Trust the Dream Builder. Let all offense and bitterness go.

# DAY 5

The LORD is my strength and my shield; my heart trusts in him,
and he helps me. —*Psalm 28:7*

You are a daughter of the Dream Builder. God is love and his Spirit is within you. When you walk in love, you are keeping in step with the Spirit—a path that will bring you into God's plan for your life.

Gear up and get ready to uncover more truth about forgiveness. God wants his love to fill you to overflowing (John 7:37–39). Stand on the truth. The truths that worked in Joseph's life will work in yours.

## Rely on the Lion of Judah

To forgive, we must rely on the Holy Spirit to live through us. To hold on to hurts is under-standable, justifiable, and natural. To get angry and want revenge is easy. But to forgive is supernatural. God has given us his resurrection power through the Holy Spirit (Ephesians 1:13, 19–20).

When Judah made his plea for Benjamin, Joseph's heart was touched (Genesis 44:18–45:1). The tears flowed. Forgiveness was complete, and the time for reconciliation had come.

Judah was willing to give his life for Benjamin. Years later, one of Judah's descendants would give his life for all of us. Jesus would come from the tribe of Judah. Jesus, the Lion of Judah (Revelation 5:5).

Only when you abide in the Lion of Judah can you bear the fruit of forgiveness. You do not have the ability to love this way on your own, but God can love through you as you abide in him. You are not alone. God never gives us a command he expects us to follow in our own strength (John 15:1–13).

A wise friend of mine once advised me that the key to truly loving others is to love out of the overflow of God's love for us. Live as if you are already loved because you are! You are God's treasure. Spend time with God, and he will fill you with his love, which will spill out to others (Romans 5:5).

For the Dream Builder to build his dream in your life, you must abide in him. To abide, you must love as Christ loved—unconditionally. You must forgive to abide, and you must abide to have the ability to forgive (John 15:1–10).

Like cold stones and other debris piled up in a river, preventing the free flow of life-giving water, layers of unforgiveness can keep the living water of the Holy Spirit from flowing through our lives. Removing the stones by abiding in Christ is essential to keep the water flowing. As we allow his love to flow freely through us, we can give life to others.

The process of clearing the pathway seems unfair and impossible with our own thinking and in our own strength. However, all things are possible with God (Luke 1:37; John 15:16). With his help, you can forgive. Forgiveness is a provision, a process, and an opportunity for beyond-measure blessings.

## Make Praise a Prayer Priority

*Judah* means "praised."[1] When Paul and Silas found themselves unjustly put in prison, they began praising God with hymns (Acts 16:25). If you find yourself in a prison of bitterness, build an altar of praise.

Spend time in praise and thankfulness for what God has done in your life. The more you reflect on your blessings, the more you will remember God can do greater things than you could ever ask (Ephesians 3:20). Praise prevents the spirit of bitterness from overtaking your soul. As you reflect and remember, rest your trust in the Dream Builder and be brave enough to let go of hurts in your life.

## Consider the Debt Jesus Paid for Us

Judah offered to take the punishment in place of Benjamin. He offered to pay his debt. This is a picture of what Jesus did for us on the cross as he stood in our place so you and I could have a relationship with God—eternally.

When I look at the sin in my life and God's grace that freely covers it all, how can I hold a debt over anyone else? When I receive God's mercy for myself, that mercy will flow to others. God's grace through Christ covers all our sin. The more we see the sin in our lives, the more we see God's grace extended to us freely and without measure. Reflecting on that should help us show grace to others (Matthew 18:21–35).

Jesus offered us grace by paying with his life for our sins. His gift of forgiveness is so much bigger than any forgiveness we may be called to extend to those who have hurt us. Pride and self-righteousness can steal our compassion for others. Stay humble! We don't deserve God's grace, but he gives it. And so we need to give grace to others, even if they don't deserve it (Ephesians 5:2).

## Confront in Love

When our hearts are truly free from any unforgiveness and full of love for the people who hurt us, we will be ready to confront them in love.

What do you learn about confronting in love from these passages, and how can you see evidence of each passage from Joseph's exchange with his brothers in Genesis 45:1–8?

Galatians 6:1–4

Ephesians 4:25–32

Matthew 18:15

Joseph's heart was free to love his brothers with no holding back. He never denied what happened or swept it under the carpet but spoke the truth to his brothers. He did not speak the truth with selfish motives—to get them to apologize or to say they were wrong. He spoke the truth to show his love for them. He spoke the truth to help his brothers and point them back to the Dream Builder.

At the promptings of the Holy Spirit, confronting others in love is healthy and beneficial for both parties. Jesus was full of grace and truth (John 1:17; 4:15–18).

Joseph released his brothers and set their minds at ease, telling them not to be distressed. Can you imagine the guilt and fear they had lived with all those years? When we confront others, it should not be to condemn them or to get something for ourselves. The goal of confronting others is to help them and point them back to God by sharing the truth.

## Rely on God's Timing for Reconciliation

Forgiveness does not necessarily equal trust or a restored relationship. Restoration may come, but forgiveness and a restored relationship are two different issues. It's important that we wait on God and allow ourselves to be led by the Spirit.

Joseph had already chosen forgiveness, but would reconciliation be the next step? He was wise. He watched his brothers and waited. Had his brothers' hearts changed? Did jealousy still reign in their lives? How had they treated his baby brother, Benjamin, in his absence? When Joseph gave his younger brother extra portions and put the cup in his sack, he was setting up a situation to see how his brothers would react.[2] When he gave Benjamin more portions than his brothers, he wanted to see how they would respond to his preferential treatment. When he sneaked Pharaoh's cup into Benjamin's sack, I believe he was not interested in trapping Benjamin. He wanted to see what was in his brothers' hearts. Would they come to Benjamin's rescue . . . or would they "throw him into a pit"?

The brothers' response revealed a heart change. There was no negative response to the extra portions. When the cup was found in Benjamin's sack, they tore their clothes, and Judah offered to take the punishment for Benjamin. I am not suggesting that it's a good idea to trick people, but I do love Joseph's wise approach.

> The brothers' hearts had changed. Sometimes this is not the case when we forgive an offender. What does Romans 12:18 teach you about your responsibility in reconciliation?

_____

_____

_____

_____

Sometimes our offender's heart is still hard. We don't have the ability to change his or her heart, but we can do our part to love and forgive.

Always forgive. Always love. Always keep in step with the promptings of the Holy Spirit. That's your part. That's what God has called you to do. Forgive in obedience to God, but don't forgive others to get them to change. You cannot make anyone change. However, when you forgive, the door opens for God to work in powerful ways.

When we wait on God, we are giving him room to work in ways we never could. If we try to force reconciliation, we are following our flesh and trying in our measured strength to do what only God can do in his unlimited greatness. Submit to God's leading as he does his perfect work. Trust him for the outcome. If you are expecting a certain response from the other person, you may find yourself once more in a state of hurt and unforgiveness.

## Have You Forgiven Yourself?

Sometimes we find it more difficult to forgive ourselves than to forgive others. Ask yourself if you are holding on to unforgiveness toward yourself. Jesus commands us to let it go. It's not holy to beat ourselves up repeatedly for mistakes, yet sometimes that is exactly what we do. Although God's mercies are new every morning, we persist in waking up each day revisiting our mistakes and hating ourselves for them (Lamentations 3:22–23). Confess your sins before God in prayer and let them go!

Jacob set himself up to be Joseph's everything. I am sure all those years as he sat in sorrow, he blamed himself for his son's alleged death. After all, he was the one who sent Joseph away to find his brothers on the day he disappeared. This led to a major victim mentality. "Everything is against me!" (Genesis 42:36). But this is never true. God is always for us (Romans 8:32–34)!

Jacob refused to forgive himself and acted out of fear instead of faith. He failed to trust God and would not let Benjamin go to Egypt with his brothers (Genesis 42:38). Simeon sat in prison while Jacob wallowed in his pit of sorrow. Woe is me. Because of Jacob's refusal to forgive himself, the blessings to his family were delayed. Imagine if he had let Benjamin go in the first place how much heartache would have been avoided.

Condemnation is one of the ways I have personally experienced torment when I could not forgive myself (Revelation 12:10). When we hold on to unforgiveness, we open a door for the enemy's torment (Matthew 18:34; Ephesians 4:26–28). Receiving God's forgiveness closes that door! Condemnation ends through confession and repentance.

Unforgiveness toward others or ourselves fixes our eyes on ourselves and takes them off Jesus. Eyes on ourselves and our mistakes, we are reluctant to receive blessings from God or help from others. Eyes on ourselves, we fail to see our blessings. Eyes on ourselves, we believe Satan's lies and fall into fear and irrational thinking.

Turn your eyes to Jesus. Self-focus of any kind is pride. Turn your eyes to Jesus. His grace is enough.

Jesus died to set you free. If you refuse to forgive yourself, you are denying his gift to you. His grace is enough, and you do not need to carry your sins around anymore. Release them to Jesus.

Failure is a part of life. But failure is in the past, and today is a new day. You can make new choices. Daughter of the Dream Builder, receive forgiveness and move on! God needs you in his army.

## What Have You Learned?

What is one new truth you learned about forgiveness this week? How will you apply it to your life?

_____

_____

_____

_____

_____

One of the most important choices you can make in life is to forgive. That command from your Dream Builder will be a part of every God-given plan. As you fill up with God's love, his love will overflow into the lives of others.

Joseph forgave and opened the door for reconciliation and restoration for generations to come (2 Corinthians 5:17–19).

Your Dream Builder loves you, and he is asking you to love others. Part of loving is forgiving. Walking in forgiveness is for your benefit. When you hold on to hurts, you put yourself in a prison. Unforgiveness affects every area of your life, including living out your God-given dream. Get up from the table of unforgiveness—it gives you nothing but grief in return. God sees your hurt and he knows your sorrows. Trust in the King of Kings to bring healing and restoration.

"The reason the Son of God appeared was to destroy the devil's work" (1 John 3:8). Don't follow the plans of the enemy, which bring destruction. Follow God's commands, which bring life to you and to others. You are a daughter of the Dream Builder. Have faith in God. Choose to walk in forgiveness and see his dream for your life come to pass.

# DAY 6

Jesus said, "Father, forgive them, for they do not know what they are doing."
*—Luke 23:34*

## She Was Powerful . . . Because She Forgave

*The wound in her soul was hidden from her eyes but not from her heart. The hurt continued to haunt her, seeping out of her soul and into her thought life. No matter how hard she tried to forget what happened, her mind automatically reached into her soul and retrieved the repressed hurt, replaying it again and again. The wound owned her, and it was growing bigger even though her offender was miles away.*

*She wanted to be free. She felt powerless.*

*"Just forgive," she heard her pastor say. "Be kind and compassionate to one another, forgiving one each other just as in Christ God forgave you" (Ephesians 4:32).*

*But what **is** forgiveness? Rather than bringing freedom to her soul, this advice often brought frustration. She was tired of being a doormat others used to wipe their feet. She had to do something. Her buried hurt was building to the point of breaking her.*

## Understanding Changes Everything

I believe one of the biggest barriers to forgiving others is not understanding what it truly means to forgive.

At odds with our human nature and often misunderstood, forgiveness is a hard concept to grasp. Easier perhaps to say what it is not: Forgiveness is *not* saying what happened was okay. Forgiveness does *not* mean forgetting what happened. Forgiveness does *not* mean trusting the person who has proven to be untrustworthy . . . but it *does* mean trusting God to handle the situation.

*Forgiveness is letting go of your right to retaliate by releasing your offender to God.*

If you retaliate, you are allowing your offender to control your life. If you repress your emotions or deny them, you'll swallow that anger and plant the seed of bitterness in your soul. Revenge, repression, retaliation . . . they all put you in a prison. *But releasing the offense to God allows the Great I AM to control your life.* With that release comes freedom.

Being real about your hurt and bringing that pain to God opens the door for healing. Showing love to your enemies dissolves your offender's power to hurt you because it confirms that God is in control of your life.

*When you release others, you open your hands to receive from God, the only One who can redeem and restore.*

God wants you to be powerful, not passive. God's power does not rest in revenge—it rests in love. Love is a powerful force that puts God in control instead of your offender. Forgiveness carves a path for the mighty river of God's love and power to flow to you—and through you to others!

The Dream Builder has a great purpose for your life. He wants you to spend your energy on your purpose—not dwelling on buried hurts or revenge. Focusing on God's purpose for your journey is an essential, effective way to live. You are not responsible for your offender's actions, but you *are* responsible for how you respond. God saw what happened to you. He is not asking you to say what happened was okay—but he does want you to turn it over to him.

## For *You* to Be Okay, You Must Treat the Wound *His* Way

When you retaliate, your offender is in control. When you respond in love and forgiveness, God is in control. Forgiveness carves a path for the mighty river of his love and power to flow.

Who will rule *your* heart? Your offender . . . or God? God never gives us a command without promising us the power to walk that truth. On your own, this love is impossible, but with God all things are possible. Don't let your offender steal your power for even one more day. Wounds are never easy to deal with. But just for today, take the first step—bring God your willing heart.

> *She told God she was ready to forgive. She didn't want to, but that was okay. God wrapped his arms around her and told her if she was willing, he would help her. It was a process. It didn't happen overnight. But when she let go of the painful relationship and released that person to God, a door opened in her soul. Redemption came in and healed the raw wound in her heart. God redeemed all that had been lost in ways beyond anything she could have ever dreamed.*

> *She was free. She was fearless. She was powerful . . . because she forgave!*

## Prepare Your Heart

You too can be fearless. You too can forgive and forge ahead into God's dream for your life. And as I write these words, know that I am on this journey with you. It takes a very brave heart to forgive. In our video this week, we are going to walk through an exercise to forgive together—but for today I just want you to spend some time with your Dream Builder in prayer.

As you pray, ask God to show you who you need to forgive and ask him to prepare your heart. Remember: if you are willing, he is able. Coming to him in prayer to ask for help is the first step. Do that today!

*Our greatest hurts can become gateways for our new beginning. Forgiveness is the key that unlocks the door.*

# VIDEO SESSION NOTES

# Chapter 6
# PRESSING ON

# DAY 1

### Nourish Scripture: Genesis 46–50

 **1 PRAY.**

Begin your time with God in prayer.

**2 MEDITATE ON GOD'S WORD.**

Using your Anchor of Truth Card* from last week's Nourish Notes, renew your mind on that truth. Quiet and focus your thoughts. Pray the truth. Say the truth. Meditate on God's truth.

**3 TAKE THE *REVEAL* STEP OF THE NOURISH BIBLE STUDY METHOD.**

Connect with Jesus by studying the Weekly Nourish Scripture and allowing the Holy Spirit to reveal truth in those verses. Prayerfully read over and reflect on the passage. Mark any phrases, verses, or words that catch your attention. Journal and learn as the Lord leads you.

---

*Anchor of Truth Cards are available at www.TreasuredMinistries.com/shop

# DAY 2

Nourish Scripture: Genesis 46–50

 **PRAY.**

Begin your time with God in prayer.

 **MEDITATE ON GOD'S WORD.**

Using your Anchor of Truth Card* from last week's Nourish Notes, renew your mind on that truth. Quiet and focus your thoughts. Pray the truth. Say the truth. Meditate on God's truth.

**TAKE THE *RESPOND* STEP OF THE NOURISH BIBLE STUDY METHOD.**

Respond to activate truth in your life. The acronym **IMPACT** provides questions to help you apply the truth from your weekly Nourish Scripture. **Sometimes you may not have answers for all six questions.**

**IMAGE OF GOD TO TRUST?** An attribute of God, Jesus, or the Holy Spirit to trust.

**MESSAGE TO SHARE?** A word of encouragement, truth, or prayer to share.

**PROMISE TO TREASURE?** A promise in the Bible to believe.

**ACTION TO TAKE?** A specific step God is calling you to take.

**CORE IDENTITY IN CHRIST TO AFFIRM?** A truth about how God sees you to affirm.

**TRANSGRESSION TO CONFESS?** A sin to acknowledge for help, healing, and restoration through Christ.

*Anchor of Truth Cards are available at www.TreasuredMinistries.com/shop

# DAY 3

Nourish Scripture: Genesis 46–50

**1 PRAY.**

Begin your time with God in prayer.

**2 MEDITATE ON GOD'S WORD.**

Using your Anchor of Truth Card* from last week's Nourish Notes, renew your mind on that truth. Quiet and focus your thoughts. Pray the truth. Say the truth. Meditate on God's truth.

**3 TAKE THE *RENEW* STEP OF THE NOURISH BIBLE STUDY METHOD.**

Like an anchor that secures its vessel, biblical meditation secures truth to transform your life. Take five minutes to *renew* your mind by focusing on one word, verse, or truth that the Holy Spirit revealed through the Bible during your week of study. Record your truth below and on your Anchor of Truth card.* Quiet your thoughts. Focus on the truth. Read the truth. Pray the truth.

**4 UTILIZE YOUR *ANCHOR OF TRUTH* CARD AS A BOOKMARK TO CULTIVATE A DAILY PRACTICE OF BIBLICAL MEDITATION.**

Place your Anchor of Truth Card* in your Bible study workbook to bookmark tomorrow's day of study. Let your Anchor of Truth bookmark remind you to pause and renew your mind on God's Word. Repeat this process daily, continuing to reflect on your Anchor of Truth to start your quiet time until the next week, when God reveals another truth to you.

*Anchor of Truth Cards are available at www.TreasuredMinistries.com/shop

# DAY 4

*Blessed are those whose strength is in you,*
*whose hearts are set on pilgrimage. —Psalm 84:5*

You have purpose. Your life was designed to bring value to this world. You are nothing less than amazing, and you matter greatly to the Dream Builder. What an astonishing truth to ponder: God desires to build his dream through you! Dust off your boots and stand on your feet, sister—God is calling his daughters to step out and follow the Holy Spirit, to live the extraordinary and leave a legacy of his love and glory through the power of the gospel.

Oh, how I hope you have been inspired to live God's purpose in life through this study. There is an enemy of our souls who would love nothing more than to convince us we are useless and defeated, but don't ever believe that lie. You are on a pilgrimage that will require persistent faith! At times you may feel hard-pressed on every side but you are never crushed when you rely on his strength (2 Corinthians 4:8). God has a dream for you. Amazing things can happen when you give control of your life over to the Dream Builder and trust him with childlike faith.

"Blessed are those whose strength is in you, whose hearts are set on pilgrimage" (Psalm 84:5). Relying on his strength, set your heart on a pilgrimage to live for God's glory and never look back. There could be no greater joy in life (Jeremiah 29:11; John 4:34; Matthew 25:19–21).

Keeping your heart set on your pilgrimage requires a determination to rely on the Dream Builder's strength through an unyielding faith. God never promises an easy road, so keep your heart set on a pilgrimage to live for God's glory no matter how difficult the road. When circumstances suggest otherwise, stand on your faith and find the courage to move forward.

You have been on a pilgrimage in your study of Joseph and the patriarchs. Today as we review our passage from this week, I want to pull out some key points we have learned together during our study.

First, let's step back into our story . . .

Joseph stood tall to present his father, Jacob, before Pharaoh. Stepping forward, Jacob leaned on his staff to support his weak hip.

"How old are you?" Pharaoh asked Jacob.

To Pharaoh he replied, "The years of my pilgrimage are a hundred and thirty. My years have been few and difficult, and they do not equal the years of the pilgrimage of my fathers" (Genesis 47:9).

Jacob described his life as a difficult pilgrimage. He knew he was nearing the end of his life. While his life had been difficult, the hardships now seemed to fade away in light of God's goodness. Jacob worshipped God while leaning on his staff to stand straight. His favorite son had been blessed and brought to a place of immense power, which he used to save the rest of his family. Jacob served a faithful God!

God never let go of Jacob. He never let go of Joseph. God was with Joseph in the pit, the prison, and finally the palace, all the while building his dream. Wise Joseph prepared, guided Egypt through a severe famine, and ultimately saved his family and God's dream through his chosen people. God never let go of the dream, the vision. Abraham, Isaac, Jacob, Joseph, and all Abraham's descendants are in a covenant relationship with God. Every believer in Christ is grafted into Abraham's family. God never leaves us. He was always with the patriarchs, and he is always with us—with you and with me. God is faithful to his promise and his Word. God will never let go of you and his dream for your life. Keep your heart set to live for his glory and watch God build his dream through you.

## Keep Your Heart Set on God to Uncover Your Unique Purpose

Our God-given dream is revealed through our relationship with our Dream Builder and set in motion as we surrender. On your pilgrimage keep in step with the Holy Spirit; God will continue to point you in the direction of your dream.

God's call on your life is personal. God called Jacob by name—and he calls you by name. You are not a speck lost among the billions of people in this world. The Dream Builder knows you by name. How has God called your name out over the course of this study?

_____

_____

_____

_____

How will you respond?

_____

_____

_____

_____

Yes, the Dream Builder delights in calling you by name and showing you his unique purpose for your life. But your dream will remain simply a revelation if you don't take action. Jacob replied quickly and decisively with three powerful words: "Here I am" (Genesis 46:2).

As you respond to your calling, remember you will be blessed with exactly what you need to fulfill your God-given dream. While each of Jacob's sons would father a tribe of Israel, their blessings would differ (Genesis 49). Each son's blessing would be unique and appropriate to him (Genesis 49:28). If Jacob, an earthly father, bestowed blessings that were just right to each of his sons, how much more will our heavenly Father give to his children (Matthew 7:9–11)?

Jacob's blessings included discipline for his sons. Yes, even God's discipline is love and prepares us for our purpose (Hebrews 12:9–13; Deuteronomy 8:2–10).

As you forge ahead on your pilgrimage, keep your eyes on what God has called you to do. Beware of jealousy. Cultivate your own gifts instead of craving another's calling or coveting another's blessing.

Rest in knowing God is weaving together all the dreams he has built, creating the tapestry of his plan. You are a treasure designed for a unique purpose (Ephesians 2:10). Connect—don't compete—with your sisters in Christ. Comparing yourself to others and their gifts is a waste of time and energy. When you strive to be someone you are not, frustration and a sense of failure will settle in. Passionately pursue your own calling and encourage others to do the same. The principle of sowing and reaping stands the test of time (Galatians 6:7–8). The more you help others develop their calling, the more you will find yourself developing yours.

## Set Your Heart on God's Path Even When You Don't Understand

Sometimes God's direction may not make any sense to you, but as you seek his presence, God will guide you where you need to go. Sometimes you will need to forge ahead without understanding the "why" or the "how" (Proverbs 3:5–6).

Jacob could have said, "Egypt? It does not make sense. That's where Abraham went and got into a heap of trouble! Lord, you said Canaan!" But instead, he stepped out and trusted God.

Jacob stopped at Beersheba to seek the Lord before he went to Egypt. However, once God gave him that word of confirmation, he never questioned the wisdom of going to Egypt again. He stood on the truth. He had faith in God's word.

It's important to seek the Lord, but then it's important to believe. To have faith in what he has said and step out in obedience. Don't waver when circumstances suggest another way and miss God's provision for your dream (Mark 4:17).

What are some negative effects of becoming "double-minded" after you seek the Lord? See James 1:4–8.

_____

_____

_____

I cannot tell you how many times I have pulled back from what I knew God was telling me to do, plagued by the what ifs. I had a "Bethel moment" recently, marked that scripture, and put it into action. But then I began to walk by sight and not by faith—and I started to doubt. *What if? Did God really say that to me? What if I can't do this?* My doubt snowballed into confusion.

Doubt is unbelief and prevents you from moving ahead on your pilgrimage. When you doubt, you become unstable and self-focused as you try to figure things out. Double-mindedness keeps you preoccupied with your circumstances instead of standing on the truth God has promised you.

As Jacob stood on the truth and journeyed to Egypt, he was blessed beyond measure. Jacob was not only reunited with Joseph but he also lived to see and bless Joseph's two sons. His family was not only saved from the famine but also thrived by living in the best part of the land (Genesis 47:5–6). This was provision for the dream God had first given Abraham so many years before. God was taking care of his people through Egypt's wealth. Sometimes our provision will come from the most unlikely places and people.

Sometimes when you step out in obedience to God, you may face persecution and hardship. If this happens, don't question your steps—and above all, don't ever question God's love for you. Part of God's provision for Joseph was the pit and prison, and they propelled Joseph into his purpose. Keep your heart set on your pilgrimage to live for his glory regardless of what happens by remembering this: his strength will carry you through any trial you face.

On your pilgrimage don't be plagued or pushed down by your past. Mistakes do not disqualify you from God's dream. There is no such thing as a perfect pilgrim. That thinking will keep you bound in needless shame and fearful of taking any steps. Don't you just love that God called Jacob by his original name? "Jacob, Jacob." Not Israel, but Jacob. "Jacob, I know you by name. I know what you were like before I changed your name and afterward. I know everything about you, and I need you to do my work—it's time to arise." God knows everything about you and needs you on his team to strengthen others by pointing them to the Dream Builder (Luke 22:31–32; John 4:39–42). Release your past to Jesus through confession! Stand tall! Repent and arise! Jesus died on the cross so you could live for him. Let go of your ashes and let God turn them into something beautiful (Isaiah 61:3).

## Set Your Heart on the Lord, Not People

Joseph's family remained shepherds, and most Egyptians viewed shepherds with disdain. This meant they needed to stay separate from the places heavily populated by Egyptians, and Pharaoh agreed with Joseph that they should live in Goshen. This separation was actually God's provision for the Israelites—a provision of protection. Had the Israelites mingled too closely with the Egyptians, they could have been unduly influenced by customs contrary to God's ways.[1]

Trust God to connect you to the right people and let go of your need to be accepted by everyone (1 Corinthians 15:33). Ask God for clarity about those he does not want you to connect with, especially those he wants you to disconnect with.

Remember Joseph! In our study we learned that Potiphar's house was not the final resting place for Joseph's God-sized dream. Pharaoh's palace would be the platform for God's purpose. The rejection from Joseph's brothers and the punishment from Potiphar's wife actually positioned him for his purpose.

Sometimes the storms of rejection send the right winds to our sails and the correct current to carry us to the right people and places at the right time.

So don't be afraid to let go of people who have let go of you. Rejection or separation can actually be a form of God's protection. As he did with Joseph and his brothers, God may reconcile a broken relationship for you if that is his will. The most important thing to remember in life is to stay inside God's will. If that means facing rejection, then remember he has something better! Don't fear rejection—fear the Lord! As long as you have God, you have everything you need (John 2:23–25).

## Set Your Heart on Living Led as a Daughter of the Dream Builder

What a beautiful scene when Jacob arose from his bed to embrace and bless Joseph's children before he died. Pulling them close, Jacob adopted Joseph's sons, Ephraim and Manasseh, into God's chosen family, giving them rights to the covenant God had made with Abraham.[2]

In our study we learned that through our faith in Christ, we become adopted children of the Dream Builder. Although you have been adopted as God's child, there is a difference between *being* God's child and *living* as God's child. Through Christ, you are not only adopted into a new family, but you are also given the indwelling of the Holy Spirit to walk in a new way of life. You must think like a daughter of the Dream Builder—by believing in his love for you and learning to trust and listen to the Holy Spirit.

As you travel through the scriptures beyond our study, use IMPACT questions from the Nourish Bible Study Method as an opportunity to hear your heavenly Father speaking

to your heart, calling you to follow in his footsteps. No step is too small to make an IMPACT—each one is significant in its own way.

## Set Your Heart on His Dream and Surrender Yours

Jacob placed his right hand on Ephraim, blessing him and placing him ahead of Manasseh even though Manasseh was the firstborn. Although Joseph protested, Jacob by faith in God's spoken word blessed the younger over the older. Jacob gently reminded Joseph that he would bless Manasseh, but in the way God intended.

Sometimes you have to surrender your dreams to find his dreams for your life.

Bring your dreams out into God's light by laying them before him in prayer, releasing each one to him (John 3:21). As you are honest before him and release each dream to him, his light will discern them for you. You don't want to follow a dream born in your flesh because you will have to sustain that dream in your own strength. A spirit-led dream has endless sustenance as the Dream Builder is behind it!

Bring your desires to him also. Sometimes our motives for our dreams are for our benefit instead of God's glory. The key is to be honest and bring everything out into the light. God will show you in his own time what to do.

God may direct you to lay down a dream for a time while he prepares your heart and redirects your desires. Before Francine Rivers wrote *Redeeming Love*, she had to surrender her gift and desire to write. Following a season of surrender, God used her gift to write for his glory.[3] The result was a novel that has pointed many broken hearts to trust God's love in greater measure.

The purpose of every God-given dream is to bring glory to God. True success in God's eyes is taking hold of God's purpose for your life by allowing the Dream Builder to take hold of you. Fulfillment will find you when you seek God and live for him. Never allow your dream to become your god. Keep your heart set on the Dream Builder.

## Guard Your Heart Through Forgiveness

Joseph continued to walk in forgiveness and bless his brothers even after Jacob passed away.

Each offense you experience will be an ongoing opportunity to release others and receive from God by turning your faith to him over and over again. You will need to continually check your heart and repeatedly let go of offense.

I love this exchange between Peter and Jesus.

> At that point Peter got up the nerve to ask, "Master, how many times do I forgive a brother or sister who hurts me? Seven?"

Jesus replied, "Seven! Hardly. Try seventy times seven." (Matthew 18:21–25 MSG)

Set your heart and keep it clean from grudges and bitterness. Rest and receive from God's strength. Trust God and not man—and watch your dream unfold.

## Onward!

You are a pilgrim; God has equipped you with plans, provision, and purpose. The road may be rough, but the journey will make you strong as you learn to lean on the Dream Builder every step of the way. See obstacles as an opportunity to build your faith as you trust God. That's how you keep your heart set on your pilgrimage. You were born to bring him glory.

### Key Treasure

Once you receive a personal revelation, don't question his provision, your position, or your purpose. Keep putting one foot in front of the other.

# DAY 5

*...to bestow on them a crown of beauty instead of ashes, the oil of joy instead of mourning, and a garment of praise instead of a spirit of despair. They will be called oaks of righteousness, a planting of the LORD for the display of his splendor. —Isaiah 61:3*

Look around you. Daughters of the Dream Builder in passionate pursuit of God's purpose for their lives are everywhere. The promises of God do not apply to only Jacob and Joseph—they belong to every believer. They belong to you.

Sadly, sometimes pain from our pilgrimages can leave us questioning God's goodness, hanging our heads in shame. But if we will surrender our pain into the palm of our Dream Builder, we can see that God will use even the broken parts of our lives and turn them into something beautiful.

Nothing inspires me to press on more than the testimony of a woman walking in her God-given purpose! Today I want to inspire you through a testimony of a dear friend of mine, Karen Rhodes.

Karen and her husband, David Rhodes, founded Kidz Konnect 4 Jesus to minister the love of Christ to the children and families in Belize. What God is building through Kidz Konnect is nothing short of a miracle. In a short time, Karen and David have become part of a large community. Their ministry includes Bible study, weekly visits to each of the schools, feeding and vitamin programs, clothing, medical clinics, discipleship, character and leadership training, camps, and other work. You can see God's glory everywhere (www.kidzkonnect4jesus.org).

One summer our family had the privilege of serving alongside Kidz Konnect at a children's sports camp. What a privilege to be a small part of encouraging the next generation of children in Belize through this ministry!

The greatest blessing I received on that mission trip was hearing Karen's story, and I want to share that blessing with you. May her story remind you that the Dream Builder can take the most painful parts of your life and use them for a greater purpose as you surrender your heart to him.

## Karen's Story

Soak in God's faithfulness as you read Karen's testimony.

Each one of us begins our journey full of promise, hope, and dreams. The women of my family are and were no different. When I was a little girl, I had a favorite patch-work quilt that I would snuggle in each night at bedtime. This quilt must have represented so many stories as each patch of cloth was painstakingly stitched by my great-grandmother. Each piece of cloth connected to the next, symbolic of the connections between generations of women.

As I think back over my life and the women God has placed in my path words such as brave, courageous, and determined come to mind . . . hardworking women of integrity.

Eventually, as all things of this world do, the quilt began to ravel and weaken with age and use. She could no longer provide the nurturing that I sought within her shreds. I began to feel exposed and isolated. So I went in search of that next object that would provide the safety and love that I desperately desired.

In my home I was the eldest child of four. My mother led the PTA and Girl Scouts and my dad was a deacon in the church. To the world we were a typical family yet something was terribly wrong. My dad had been brought up in a family where his father was abusive and my father claimed this same sin for his generation . . . sexually abusing his children.

The search for my new protector took me on a journey. I would climb through the back of my closet into the attic filled with pink fluffy clouds of insulation and heat. Now mind you, this compared not to the Wardrobe in Narnia. However, Absalom (God) met me there time and time again. The Lord would whisper into my heart that I was HIS treasure and that one day HE had a very special purpose for my life. The Lord has whispered these words into my heart my whole life. When I was ten years old I stood beside my best friend and declared my faith for my God.

It was during these years amongst the quiet pink clouds that God taught me to dream. Dreaming was out of necessity; it meant survival and was preparation for more than I could ever imagine. I wish I could say that after I claimed God as my redeemer that I became an obedient child that never strayed from the path chosen for my life and purpose, but I would be fabricating to do so. I lived numerous years with self-hatred and depression. Countless times had it not been for God's grace and mercy I shudder to think of the dreams that would have been discarded all for the lies of darkness. Maybe you can relate, "You're worthless, stupid, and unfit for God to utilize for anything." I fall to my face in gratitude for a heavenly Father that continued to love me unconditionally as I desperately ached and grieved for all that I had suffered and lost. I chose to see the darkness instead of the light. To see the impossible instead of "I'm" possible.

Eventually, God spoke his truth into my heart that in Him I live, move, and have my being, and that I am His offspring (Acts 17:28). Oh sweet daughters of Christ, please hear me, He alone takes the most threadbare and tattered to do the greatest of things.

You see, eight years ago the Lord burdened my heart for the people of Belize, especially her children. My husband, David, and I are the founders of Kidz Konnect 4 Jesus. We are the hands and feet of our Lord … a voice for generations of hopeless. This is a ministry that dares to dream God-sized dreams. To think all these years God has been taking the tattered and beautiful moments of my journey and stitching them together for his glorious purpose. And it all began with a tattered and torn quilt made with love.

## Surrendered and Persistent

The God who built his dream through Karen and Joseph is the same God who can take that passion he has placed in your heart and build his dream through you. Your pain can be transformed into your purpose! The God of Abraham, Isaac, Jacob, and Joseph is your God too.

You have a decision to make today. Will you blame God for the broken parts of your life, or will you trust in him to rebuild it so you can live his dream for your life? Even your mistakes can become your ministry! The Dream Builder already has the plans. All you have to do is surrender, trust, and hold his hand through every step.

*You are a treasure designed for a unique purpose*. He has chosen you to bear fruit beyond measure for his glory (John 15:16). May Karen's story inspire you to align your life with God's purpose and allow the Dream Builder to take control.

Listen, do you hear it? The heartbeat of the Holy Spirit is within you. Surrender. Trust. Follow. God wants to build his dream through you.

## Key Treasure

You have a decision to make today. Will you blame God for the broken parts of your life, or will you trust in him to rebuild it so you can live his dream for your life? Even your mistakes can become your ministry! The Dream Builder already has the plans. All you have to do is surrender, trust, and hold his hand through every step.

# DAY 6

Now we who have believed enter that rest.
—*Hebrews 4:3*

They carried his embalmed body to Canaan. A procession of prestigious Egyptians and all Pharaoh's officials accompanied Joseph and his family to lay Jacob to rest in the land God promised to Abraham.

In the last moments of Jacob's life, he sought Joseph's solemn promise. "Promise that you will show me kindness and faithfulness. Do not bury me in Egypt, but when I rest with my fathers, carry me out of Egypt and bury me where they are buried" (Genesis 47:29–30). Burying Jacob in the Promised Land not only honored his last request, but also revealed Jacob's faith in the Dream Builder and in God's dream for his chosen people (Genesis 15:18–21). He settled the matter privately with Joseph and then publicly with the whole family, solidifying his wishes. Jacob was now ready to rest. Looking forward to his heavenly home, the pilgrim breathed his last (Hebrews 11:13).

After burying his father in the cave of the field, Machpelah near Mamre (a field Abraham had bought in full faith of the dream), Joseph returned with his brothers and family to Egypt. Jacob's family—God's family—prospered. They were fruitful in all dimensions of life. And the dream lived on.

Years later at the end of Joseph's pilgrimage, with his brothers gathered around him, Joseph's last request echoed his father's.

> "I am about to die. But God will surely come to your aid and take you up out of this land to the land he promised on oath to Abraham, Isaac and Jacob." And Joseph made the Israelites swear an oath and said, "God will surely come to your aid, and then you must carry my bones up from this place." (Genesis 50:24–25)

Jacob and Joseph's burial requests reflected a belief in their God-given purpose and dream. Even though they could not see it, they continued to press on to their Promised Land.

Joseph breathed his last, and his body was embalmed and placed in a coffin (Genesis 50:24). As more years passed, power in Egypt would change hands, and the Israelites would be enslaved by the Egyptians. Years later, God sent Moses to deliver the Israelites from slavery in Egypt and bring them into their Promised Land, his dream fulfilled for their lives. As God's chosen people left Egypt, they carried Joseph's bones with them through the wilderness for forty years (Exodus 13:19). After securing the Promised Land, they finally laid Joseph's bones to rest as he had requested (Joshua 24:32).

Scholars believe the presence of Joseph's body waiting to be taken to the Promised Land brought hope to God's chosen people that Egypt was not their final resting place, and that God's dream for them would come to pass (Hebrews 11:22).[4]

Sometimes the seeds we sow in this generation will not reach harvest until generations to come. But we must always remember to rest in faith in our Dream Builder, and in his dream. We never labor in vain.

> Therefore, my dear brothers and sisters, stand firm. Let nothing move you. Always give yourselves fully to the work of the Lord, because you know that your labor in the Lord is not in vain. (1 Corinthians 15:58)

You are a daughter of the Dream Builder. Your life was built to bring God glory. Continue to press on to your Promised Land.

## The Promised Land Is a Place of Rest

Between Egypt and the Promised Land was a region known as the wilderness.

The wilderness is that place between receiving your call from God and living the dream. In the wilderness you must continue to press on by faith regardless of what you see. This is accomplished by believing in God's amazing, unconditional love for you. Our trust in the Lord is birthed out of his love for us.

Sadly, the Israelites spent forty years wandering around in the wilderness for what should have been an eight-day journey to the Promised Land because of their lack of trust in the Lord (Deuteronomy 1:1–3; Hebrews 3:19). They whined and complained, they made idols, and they doubted God's protection and plan in their lives. They even began to pine for Egypt (Numbers 14:1–4). Most could not even enter the Promised Land because of their unbelief (Numbers 14:20–24).

Whining when you are waiting to see God's purposes come to pass in your life will simply leave you wandering aimlessly. Choose to trust God. Imagine never seeing God's dream in your life come to pass because of unbelief! Press in and praise God by realizing this is all part of his purpose. Rejoice knowing that, like Jacob and Joseph, God will fulfill every promise to you.

When you don't understand where you are headed, when you are waiting and watching, choose to trust God by resting in his love for you. Whatever you do, don't ever give up on the Dream Builder! Know he has the perfect plan (Jeremiah 29:11; Ephesians 2:10). The enemy would love for you to retreat and walk away from your purpose! He will try his hardest. *If I can just get her to doubt God's love and his dream for her life, she will give up and walk away! If she doesn't trust God, she will be disconnected from the Dream Builder and the dream.* Don't stand for that one minute! Allow the force of your faith in God's love for you to override any fear or unbelief, and continue to press on to your Promised Land! While you are waiting ... God is working.

## Never Doubt God's Unconditional Love

Jacob's death brought sorrow within the family—and fear. Perhaps it began with just one brother, but whatever the reason, the *what ifs* surfaced, and the fear and doubt spread. "What if Joseph holds a grudge against us and pays us back for all the wrongs we did to him?" (Genesis 50:15).

Joseph wept and reassured his brothers of his love.

> "Don't be afraid. Am I in the place of God? You intended to harm me, but God intended it for good to accomplish what is now being done, the saving of many lives. So then, don't be afraid. I will provide for you and your children." And he reassured them and spoke kindly to them. (Genesis 50:19–21)

As the tears flowed, those kind words of love spoken over Joseph's brothers brought peace and rest to their souls.

**"Don't be afraid."**

Joseph was heartbroken that his brothers did not believe in his love for them. Apparently, for seventeen years they had believed his kindness was only because of his father. They believed that for his father's sake Joseph had held back his vengeance until Jacob died.

Warren Wiersbe draws a great parallel. He notes in his commentary that just as Joseph's brothers did not take him at his word, which led to fear and unbelief, Christians can fail to take God at his word and feel hopeless and abandoned. He writes this:

> When you doubt God's Word, you soon begin to question God's love, and then you give up all hope for the future, because faith, hope, and love go together. But it all begins with faith.[5]

If Joseph, with a measured ability to love, was heartbroken to hear his brothers doubted his unconditional love, imagine how the Dream Builder feels when we don't trust his love for us.

**"Am I in the place of God? You intended to harm me, but God intended it for good to accomplish what is now being done, the saving of many lives."**

Often when we have heard God's call and left our "Egypt" but are not yet in the "Promised Land," we can feel out of control and insecure because of the wilderness, the unknown— but this provides the perfect opportunity to trust God. When we try to grasp control of our lives, we are trying to take the place of God. Our role is to trust in his love, surrender our all to him, and then follow the leading of the Holy Spirit.

**"And he reassured them and spoke kindly to them."**

At the end of their pilgrimages, Joseph and Jacob gave their last requests to their family. We are closing our pilgrimage together as we close this study of Joseph and the patriarchs, and I would like to give my final words to you.

You have one life to live. Live it with purpose. His purpose. Your heart for his glory.

Give God the rightful place in your heart. As his child, you will never experience any hardship that cannot be used for his glory. Rest in his unconditional, without-measure love for you. His love will bring trust, surrender, and finally obedience as you stand in awe of a mighty God.

Let go and let God build the dream.

You were built to bring meaning to this world. You were designed and destined to do great works for his glory (see Ephesians 2:10).

The patriarchs were pilgrims and so are you! Like Abraham, Isaac, Jacob, and Joseph, you are blessed to be a blessing to others as you follow God's plan, rely on his provision, and live for his purpose. May you rest in faith in God's love and have the courage to believe in his dream for your life.

Zig Ziglar lived his life by inspiring others to find their purpose and live it with passion. There is a quote from him that I love. Let it soak in.

> You are one person in this great big world, but you were created to occupy a unique place. Right now, your chair is empty because you're struggling with whether it's worth trying to fill. But no one else can or will. If you don't grab hold of the purpose God created you to achieve it will be a tragedy! We, the rest of us, need you to accomplish your divine purpose.[6]

It's true. We need you.

Do something now.

I dare you.

I dare you to move into your God-given dream as Joseph did. I dare you to live the adventure by listening to the Holy Spirit. I dare you to lose your life—yourself—and find what is important: loving others with his love and serving others with his strength. I dare you to embrace the reality that God can use you to save the lives of many.

Are you walking in step with your God-given destiny? When you do, you can set the world on fire with God's love and make a difference.

Onward, pilgrim. The Dream Builder is calling you.

## Let Us Pray …

*I am a daughter of the Dream Builder. He has chosen me to be his child (John 1:12), ambassador (2 Corinthians 5:20), and princess (Galatians 4:7; 1 Peter 2:9).*

*I am his treasure, designed for a unique purpose (Deuteronomy 14:2; 1 Peter 2:9; Ephesians 2:10).*

*His love for me is unconditional and endless (John 3:16; 1 John 3:1; Ephesians 3:18), and his power is made perfect in all my weaknesses (2 Corinthians 12:9–10).*

*In Christ, I am completely accepted and in right standing with my heavenly Father (Galatians 2:21; Ephesians 1:4–5).*

*Father, I praise you for your grace (Ephesians 1:7) and your favor (Psalm 5:12) that surround me. Thank you, God, for the treasure of your resurrection power living inside me (Ephesians 1:19–20; 2 Corinthians 4:7).*

*I worship you as my healer (Matthew 8:17), my restorer (Psalm 23:3), and my Dream Builder. You alone are God, and you are good. You are for me (Romans 8:31), and I can overcome because Christ overcame (1 John 5:4). I am redeemed (1 Peter 1:18–19). I was created for your glory (Ephesians 2:10). I am a new creation; the old has gone and the new has come (2 Corinthians 5:17).*

*Open my eyes wide to the dream you have for my life. I trust your love and surrender my steps, big and small, that Christ may live through me. I choose today to listen to your voice above all others. I am ready to cut new paths—blazing a trail for your glory, resting in your strength. Give me the courage to believe I am your treasure, and give me the commitment to follow you so I can be a channel of your love as I live for you alone. Amen.*

# VIDEO SESSION NOTES

**Session 6**
**PRESSING ON**
*Genesis 46–50*

Videos located online at www.nourishbiblestudyseries.com

# SOURCE NOTES

### Chapter 1: THE DREAM

1. Jon Courson, *Jon Courson's Application Commentary Old Testament Volume I: Genesis-Job* (Nashville, Tenn.: Thomas Nelson, 2005), 136.

### Chapter 2: CALL ON HIS NAME

1. Angie Smith, *What Women Fear* (Nashville, Tenn.: B and H Publishing Group, 2011), 59.
2. Dictionary and word search for *Yisra'el* (Strong's 3478). *Blue Letter Bible.* www.blueletter bible.org/lang/lexicon/lexicon.cfm? Strongs=H3478&t=KJV (accessed November 2012).
3. Jon Courson, *Jon Courson's Application Commentary*, 161.
4. "Names of God," *1906 Jewish Encyclopedia.* JewishEncyclopedia.com. www.jewish encyclopedia.com/articles/11305-names-of-god (October 2012).

### Chapter 4: HER HEART FOR HIS GLORY

1. Jon Courson, *Jon Courson's Application Commentary*, 181–182.
2. Edward T. Welch, *When People Are Big and God Is Small: Overcoming Peer Pressure, Codependency, and the Fear of Man* (Phillipsburg, NJ: P & R Publishing, 1997).
3. Welch, *When People Are Big*.
4. Welch, *When People Are Big*, 61.
5. Dictionary and word search for *kardia* (Strong's 2588). *Blue Letter Bible.* www.blueletter bible.org/ lang/lexicon/lexicon.cfm?Strongs=G2588&t=KJV (accessed October 11, 2011).
6. *Be Transformed: Discovering Biblical Solutions to Life's Problems* (Oklahoma City: Scope Ministries International, Inc., 2007), 7–21.
7. Zig Ziglar, *Better Than Good* (Nashville: Integrity, 2006), 111.

### Chapter 5: RECONCILIATION

1. Dictionary and word search for *Yĕhuwdah* (Strong's 3063). *Blue Letter Bible.* www.blueletter bible.org/lang/lexicon/lexicon.cfm?Strongs=H3063&t=KJV, (accessed November 2012).
2. Jon Courson, *Jon Courson's Application Commentary*, 192.

### Chapter 6: PRESSING ON

1. Jon Courson, *Jon Courson's Application Commentary*, 201.
2. Warren Wiersbe, *The Wiersbe Bible Commentary* (Colorado Springs, Colo.: David C Cook, 2007), 135.
3. Francine Rivers, *Redeeming Love* (Sisters, Or.: Multnomah, 1997).
4. Courson, *Jon Courson's Application Commentary*, 227.
5. Wiersbe, *The Wiersbe Bible Commentary*, 141–42.
6. Zig Ziglar, *Better Than Good*, 170.

# PRAYER REQUESTS

# PRAYER REQUESTS

_____
_____
_____
_____
_____
_____
_____
_____
_____
_____
_____
_____
_____
_____
_____
_____
_____
_____
_____

# PRAYER REQUESTS

Made in the USA
Middletown, DE
12 November 2019